RUNNING RIOT

A Farcical Comedy in Three Acts

by Derek Benfield

samuelfrench.co.uk

Copyright © 1958, 1961, 1968, 1975, 1980 by Derek Benfield
All Rights Reserved

RUNNING RIOT is fully protected under the copyright laws of the British Commonwealth, including Canada, the United States of America, and all other countries of the Copyright Union. All rights, including professional and amateur stage productions, recitation, lecturing, public reading, motion picture, radio broadcasting, television and the rights of translation into foreign languages are strictly reserved.

ISBN 978-0-573-11393-2

www.samuelfrench.co.uk
www.samuelfrench.com

FOR AMATEUR PRODUCTION ENQUIRIES

UNITED KINGDOM AND WORLD
EXCLUDING NORTH AMERICA
plays@samuelfrench.co.uk
020 7255 4302/01

Each title is subject to availability from Samuel French,
depending upon country of performance.

CAUTION: Professional and amateur producers are hereby warned that *RUNNING RIOT* is subject to a licensing fee. Publication of this play does not imply availability for performance. Both amateurs and professionals considering a production are strongly advised to apply to the appropriate agent before starting rehearsals, advertising, or booking a theatre. A licensing fee must be paid whether the title is presented for charity or gain and whether or not admission is charged.

No one shall make any changes in this title for the purpose of production. No part of this book may be reproduced, stored in a retrieval system, or transmitted in any form, by any means, now known or yet to be invented, including mechanical, electronic, photocopying, recording, videotaping, or otherwise, without the prior written permission of the publisher. No one shall upload this title, or part of this title, to any social media websites.

The right of Derek Benfield to be identified as author of this work has been asserted in accordance with Section 77 of the Copyright, Designs and Patents Act 1988.

Running Riot

This play was first presented by the Salisbury Arts Theatre Company at the New Theatre, Hull, on 1st July, 1957, with the following cast of characters:—

NICOLETTE	Annette Milsom
FELIX	James Cossins
AGNES PODMORE	Margaret Jones
BASIL TRENT	Graham Armitage
BRUCHIK	Ian Gane
MISS HACKET	Ann Way
HUMPHREY PODMORE	Ronald Magill
PAULINE MARYOT	Mary Yeomans
A VISITOR	Derek Smee

Directed by THE AUTHOR
Setting designed and painted by RICHARD MARKS
Guitar music played by PETER ROSATI

The action of the play takes place at L'Auberge Blanche, a small hotel somewhere in Europe, during the time of the Olympic Games.

ACT ONE
Late afternoon on a day in summer

ACT TWO
The following morning

ACT THREE
The next day. Early afternoon

All characters and events are fictitious. Any similarity between these and any other Olympic Games, past, present or future, is entirely unintentional and extremely unlikely.

NOTE: *The running time of this play, excluding intervals, is approximately one hour and forty-five minutes.*

PRODUCTION NOTE

IN farce, the situations may be forgiven for being improbable, provided the characters caught up in them are themselves real. In RUNNING RIOT a rather pathetic little Yorkshire greengrocer, fleeing to Europe in defiance of his domineering wife, finds himself involved in the Olympic Games and is mistaken for a star athlete from whom big things are expected in the 5,000 metres. In addition to this, he is caught up in the devious world of espionage. His efforts to extricate himself from both these situations and, at the same time to escape from his pursuing wife, should provide plenty of scope for laughter.

Humphrey Podmore is the "little man" upon whose head the misfortunes are piled, and who, of course, triumphs in the end. He should be played sincerely, and with that touch of pathos which always heightens comedy. Basil Trent is a rogue; but a charming, amusing and lovable rogue. Although he is responsible for a great deal of Humphrey's discomfort, he never for a moment loses our sympathy. Basil and Humphrey must be completely opposite in temperament: Basil, on the one hand, gay, polished and confident; Humphrey, shy, pathetic and troubled.

Felix is middle-aged, a kindly, well-meaning but slightly ineffectual man. His daughter, Nicolette, is a bright, pretty teenager, and must be played with plenty of sparkle. The scenes between these two are not farcical, and must be played gently—a welcome respite from the broader moments of the play. They both speak with "mid-European" accents.

Miss Hacket and Mrs. Podmore should contrast as much as possible, both physically and vocally. Hacket is a small, wiry woman. She is very athletic, and should appear to be constantly on the move as she limbers up; knees bending, running on the spot, etc. Agnes, on the other hand, is a heavy, buxom woman with a loud voice and plenty of attack.

Bruchik is large, dark, bearded and Russian. It is important, though, not to overdo the sinister aspect or he will step outside the bounds of reality. Pauline must be beautiful. That is the first consideration when casting her, but the part (by no means an easy one) needs also a fair amount of acting. The part of the real runner—the "Visitor"—can be very rewarding, although it is only small. The drunk scene with Agnes is one of the highlights of the play, and should be played in that very slow, serious manner. He is a perky little man, wholly unconcerned and not at all surprised by what has befallen him.

In the first production of this play we used a considerable amount of guitar music. For example, at the opening of Act One, we had an unseen voice out below the balcony singing a bright French song with guitar accompaniment which helped to set a nice Continental atmosphere. We also used snatches of suitable guitar music behind some of the slower scenes, notably the ones between Nicolette and Felix in Act Three (pp. 71 and 81). This music is not, of course, essential, but if you are lucky enough to have an accomplished guitarist handy it is a decided advantage. Or you could no doubt select a suitable recording from your local supplier of this or any other instrument, such as the accordion or zither, to suggest a Continental atmosphere.

RUNNING RIOT is a light-hearted play which can be a lot of fun for both actors and audience provided it is sent along at a spanking pace. Good luck with *your* production!

DEREK BENFIELD

CHARACTERS

in order of their appearance

NICOLETTE

FELIX

AGNES PODMORE

BASIL TRENT

BRUCHIK

MISS HACKET

HUMPHREY PODMORE

PAULINE MARYOT

A VISITOR

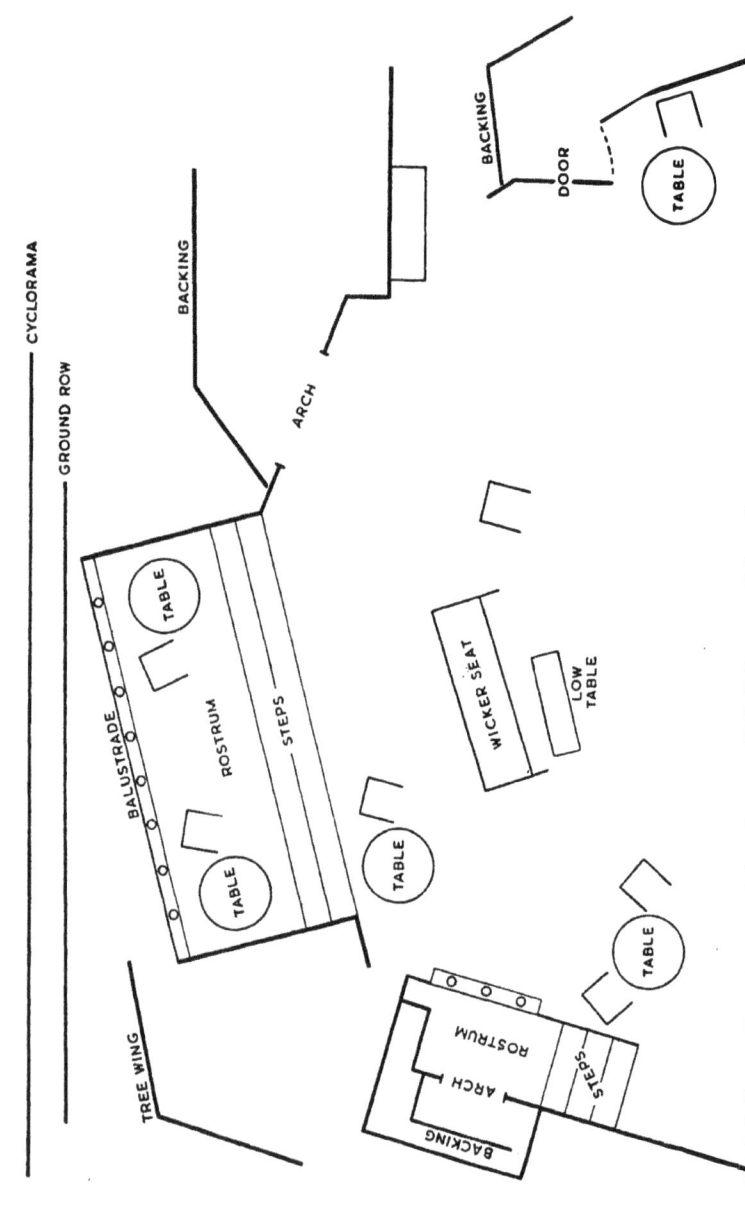

*RUNNING RIOT

ACT ONE

L'Auberge Blanche, a small hotel somewhere in Europe. Late afternoon on a day in summer.

Directly U.C. *two steps lead up on to a balcony which extends from* U.R. *to* U.L.C. *and above which is a gaily-coloured awning. There is a balustrade beyond which we can see a mountain landscape and a very blue sky. An archway* U.L. *leads through a courtyard to the main entrance of the hotel. Below this at* L.C. *is a way off by an open flat to the kitchen, and a door* D.L. *leads down into the wine cellar. There is a short flight of steps* R.C. *leading up on to a rostrum and off through an archway to the bedrooms. There is also a way off* U.R. *A fairly long wicker seat is set* C. *with a low coffee table in front of it,* L. *of which is a chair. There are five small matching round tables: one below the door* D.L. *with a chair* L. *of it; one* R.C. *with a chair either side of it; one* U.R. *with a chair* L. *of it; and one at either end of the balcony, each with one chair. If possible all this furniture should be made of wicker. There is a serving table covered by a white cloth against the open flat* L.C., *on which is the hotel register. Above this on the wall is a framed sign reading: "Every cloud has a silver lining". Two hanging lanterns, one over the archway* U.L., *the other* L. *of the archway* R.C. *There a few potted flowers against the rostrum* R.C., *and various other hanging plants about the place.*

The set should be painted in a light colour to give a very bright clean appearance, and the cushions, table cloths, etc., should be colourful and gay.

> *When the curtain rises* NICOLETTE, *a pretty young girl of nineteen, is sitting on the wicker seat* C. *She is reading a magazine and humming a gay little song. She is dressed in a full skirt, a gay off-the-shoulder blouse, flat shoes, and a tiny white apron.*

> *After a moment or two,* FELIX *comes in from the cellar door* L. *with an armful of bottles. He is a warm-hearted, lovable but slightly ineffectual man in his late forties. They both speak with a mid-European accent.*

*It is illegal to perform this play, in any circumstances whatsoever, without a licence. Please refer, for full details, to Copyright Notice preceding main text. Copyright Act (1956.)

FELIX. Nicolette!

(*At the sound of his voice* NICOLETTE *jumps up and takes knives and forks to the table* D.R.)

What are you doing?

NICOLETTE. I am preparing the tables.

FELIX (*above table* D.L.). Yes. *Now* you are preparing the tables but a moment ago you were doing nothing. You could have helped me to bring up the wine from the cellar.

NICOLETTE. I'm sorry, Papa.

FELIX (*putting down bottles on side table* L.). There is a great deal to be done before the rest of the visitors arrive this evening. (*Mopping brow and moving to below table* C.) Your mother chose a very good time to go and spend a few days with her sister in Alsace! The first time we have been full for many years.

NICOLETTE. Why do you pretend that we are full up, Papa? There are plenty of rooms.

FELIX. Because after tonight I think we *shall* be full up. It is all psychological. If you think you are doing badly, you will do badly. But if you think you are doing well, then you will do well.

NICOLETTE. A pity we cannot have the Olympic Games here every year, then we should have a good chance of always being full up.

FELIX. Now, I want you to remember, Nicolette, that you are to behave yourself when these people are here. Some of them are very important.

NICOLETTE (*to* R. *of* FELIX). I thought the important people were staying at the *big* hotel down the road?

FELIX (*grudgingly*). Well—er—well, yes, some of them are. (*With sudden determination.*) But there are important people staying *here*, too! This is a very important hotel! (*To door* D.L.)

NICOLETTE (*with a smile, humouring him*). Yes, Papa. Of course it is. (*She tidies table* C.)

(FELIX *closes and locks the cellar door.*)

FELIX (*moving up from door* D.L.). Now, Nicolette, you must try to speak the very good English for the British runner when he arrives.

NICOLETTE. Yes, Papa.

FELIX. It is an honour for us to have him staying here, remember.

NICOLETTE. Yes, Papa.

(*He takes down a sign that is hanging on the wall above the hotel register and moves to* L. *of* NICOLETTE.)

FELIX. You see the sign I have put up here? "Every cloud has a silver lining." I thought that would make the English feel at home.

(*He returns the notice to its original position.* NICOLETTE *takes knives and forks to table* U.R. *and lays it for one.*)

NICOLETTE (*after a pause*). Did you get your letter, Papa?
FELIX (*his face falls*). Oh, yes, I did.
NICOLETTE. Was it not good news?
FELIX (*to* D.L. *of* C. *table*). I have two weeks in which to pay the money I owe. If I do not then they will close the hotel.
NICOLETTE (*coming down to below table* C.). But the hotel is doing better now.
FELIX. Yes, but it will take a little time to get back the money I have lost. In three, four or five months I could repay the loan. But in two weeks—it is impossible.
NICOLETTE (*moves to* R. *of* FELIX *and touches his arm*). Do not worry. Something will turn up.
FELIX (*brightening suddenly and crossing below her to* C.). Whatever happens, we must make everyone very welcome.
NICOLETTE. How do you mean, Papa?
FELIX. Whenever somebody appears we must rush out to them and say "Bonjour, bonjour, bonjour!"
NICOLETTE. Why do we speak to them in French?
FELIX. Everybody understands French! We say to them: "Bonjour, bonjour, bonjour! Welcome to L'Auberge Blanche!"
NICOLETTE. We say "Bonjour" three times?
FELIX. With "Bonjour" once is not enough. With three times there is no doubt.
NICOLETTE (*to table* D.L. *with cutlery for one*). Why not say *everything* three times, then?
FELIX. Do not be silly, Nicolette! Then we can add, "We are honoured"—because we *are* honoured. "We are thrilled"—because we must *appear* to be thrilled.
NICOLETTE. I shall not be able to remember all that.
FELIX. You must try. Now go along and see that everything is all right in the kitchen.
NICOLETTE. All right, Papa.

(*She collects her tray from table* C. *and goes off* L.C.

He begins to rehearse quietly D.R.C. *During this* AGNES PODMORE *comes in* U.L., *unseen by* FELIX, *and watches his performance. She is a large, buxom woman of forty-five. She speaks with a North Country dialect.*)

FELIX. Bonjour! Bonjour! Bonjour! Welcome to L'Auberge Blanche! We are honoured! We are thrilled! Bonjour! Bonjour! Bonjour!

AGNES (*moving in to* C.). Why are you talking to yourself?
  (FELIX *swings round quickly, a little embarrassed.*)

FELIX. Oh, madam! I beg your pardon.

AGNES. What for? You haven't insulted me.

FELIX (*to her* R.). Bonjour! Bonjour! Bonjour! Welcome to L'Auberge—

AGNES. All right! I don't want to hear it all over again. (*She puts her handbag on table* C.)

FELIX. I was only going to say "We are honoured! We—"

AGNES. I know all that. I heard it the first time.

FELIX. You have a reservation?

AGNES. Of course not. What do you think I am—a Red Indian? (*She breaks* L. *slightly, looking about.*)

FELIX. You have booked a room?

AGNES. Not yet.

FELIX. We are very full up.

AGNES. You don't *look* very full up to me.

FELIX. Everybody is out or asleep.

AGNES (*to* L. *of him*). Have you got a little bald man staying here?

FELIX. What is his name?

AGNES. Podmore. Humphrey Podmore. Though I expect he's calling himself Smith by now.

FELIX. Ah! we have six Smiths!

AGNES. You don't surprise me. Six Smiths and no Podmore, eh?

FELIX. I do not think so, madame.

AGNES. You'd remember him if you'd seen him. I'll call back. He may turn up later. I've traced him as far as this area.

FELIX. You are a detective?

AGNES. In a way. I'm his wife.

FELIX. Oh, I see.

AGNES. I wonder if you do. Here's his card. (*She hands him a visiting card.*)

FELIX. Thank you. (*Reading.*) Humphrey Podmore.

AGNES. If he turns up, keep him here till I get back. Got it?

FELIX. Yes.

AGNES. Good.
>   (AGNES *goes abruptly* U.L. *He looks after her for a moment, bewildered. Then he takes the visiting card and puts it down near the register* L.C. *He looks in the register.*)

FELIX (*to the archway*). Ah! Mr. Podmore! Madame! It is here. Oh, well.
>   (*He shrugs and goes indoors off* L.C., *calling* "Nicolette!")
>   *After a moment* BASIL TRENT *comes on from the main entrance. He is a bright, sporty young man in his thirties. He carries a briefcase.*
>   BASIL *looks around, sees the motto on the wall, reads it and reacts. He turns its face to the wall. He idly picks up the visiting card from beside the register, and moves* C., *reading the card.*
>   FELIX *returns from* L. *in a hurry.* BASIL, *in his preoccupation with* FELIX, *keeps the card in his hand.*)

FELIX (*to* C. *with a flourish*). Ah, monsieur! Bonjour! Bonjour! Bonjour! We are delighted to welcome you to L'Auberge Blanche. It is a pleasure to have you stay with us. We are honoured! We are thrilled! Bonjour! Bonjour! Bonjour!

BASIL. All right, all right! Don't overdo it. Where am I?

FELIX. Why—L'Auberge Blanche, of course.

BASIL. Why do you say "Of course"? It didn't look very *blanche* to me outside. Parts of it were distinctly *noire*. (*To* L. *of table* D.R.)

FELIX (*to* L. *of* BASIL). Shall I take you to your room, m'sieur?

BASIL. What for?

FELIX. Perhaps you would like to see it.

BASIL. Why should I want to see it? I hate looking at strange rooms.

FELIX. It is not a strange room, m'sieur.

BASIL. Well, it is to me. (*He sits* L. *of table* D.R., *and looks at* FELIX *with rapt attention.*) What's it like?

FELIX (*bewildered*). M'sieur?

BASIL. This room. Tell me about it.

FELIX. Well, it has four walls.

BASIL. Is that all?

FELIX (*eager to please*). A ceiling.

BASIL. That's better.

FELIX. And a floor.

BASIL. Four walls, a ceiling and a floor, eh?

FELIX (*delighted*). Yes, m'sieur!

BASIL. Sounds a very ordinary room to me.

FELIX. Oh, it is! It is! An ordinary room!

BASIL (*rising*). Well, if it's an ordinary room I don't want to see it, do I? (*Realizes he still has the visiting card and hands it to* FELIX.) Oh, here you are.

FELIX. Thank you, m'sieur. (*Crossing to* C., *reading the card.*) Ah! (*To register* L.C.)

BASIL (*moving up to look over the balcony* U.R.C.). I shall want a double room.

FELIX (*getting the register*). But you have only booked a single room.

BASIL. What are you talking about? I haven't booked *any* room.

FELIX (*taking the register up to* L. *of* BASIL, *eagerly*). Oh, yes! Oh, yes!

BASIL (*escaping below* FELIX *towards the archway*). Go away! (*As* FELIX *follows him.*) Stop following me about.

FELIX (*to* R. *of* BASIL). Here is your name in the register.

BASIL. Well, it's about time. What?

FELIX (*pointing*). There! There!

BASIL. Stop saying everything twice. I don't think I like you. (*Takes the register and studies it.*)

FELIX. Can you see?

BASIL. Of course I can see! I can see, but I can't read. Why don't you learn to write?

FELIX. It would not help if monsieur cannot read.

BASIL. That's enough of that! If you could write, I could read. (*Hands back the register.*) This isn't me.

FELIX. No.

BASIL. No. Nothing like me. (*Moving below* FELIX *to* D.C.) My name is Basil Trent.

FELIX. Not Podmore?

BASIL. Podmore? Certainly not. Now, you book me a double room. (*As* FELIX *hesitates.*) What's the matter?

FELIX. But monsieur, we are very full up. (*Gestures hopelessly at the register.*)

BASIL. Have you got a double room?

FELIX. Yes, m'sieur.

BASIL. Is there anybody sleeping in it?

FELIX. No, m'sieur.

BASIL. Well, there is now.

FELIX. Very good. (*Writing in the register.*) Monsieur will be sleeping alone?

BASIL. Certainly not. Mrs. Trent will be sleeping with me.

FELIX (*at* L.C.). Mrs. Trent?

BASIL. Yes. That's my married name as well as my maiden name.
FELIX. She is your wife?
BASIL (*to* R. *of* FELIX). Look, I don't think I like your questions! Come to think of it, I don't like *you*. And I don't think I want to stay in your hotel after all! Bonjour!

(*He starts to go.* NICOLETTE *comes in from* L. *and walks across in front of* BASIL *and goes off up the stairs* R. *He watches her with delight, and then turns to* FELIX, *and puts down his briefcase.*)

All right. Where do I sign?

(FELIX *rushes to get pen from side table.*)

FELIX. That is better.
BASIL (*moving to* C., *looking after* NICOLETTE). Yes, it is! *Much* better!

(FELIX *comes to* L. *of* BASIL *with register and pen.* BASIL, *without looking, takes the pen and signs his name in error on* FELIX'S *hand. Both react.*)

I'm so sorry. (*Signs the register correctly.*)
FELIX. Where is your luggage, m'sieur?
BASIL (*picking up briefcase*). It's here. This is it.
FELIX (*taking it from him*). But that is such a little luggage! Where is ze main luggage?
BASIL. Ze main luggage?
FELIX. Ze *big* luggage.
BASIL. Oh—ze *big* luggage! Well, I left that behind. It's being sent on later.
FELIX. And your wife?
BASIL. Oh, I—er—I left *her* behind, too.
FELIX. That was very forgetful of you, m'sieur.
BASIL. Yes. One of these days I shall forget something important.
FELIX (*crossing to* D.R.C., *very seriously*). I will go and see to your room.
BASIL. Well, don't say it like that.
FELIX. Like what?
BASIL. As if you were going to set fire to it or something.
FELIX (*going upstairs*). Oh, you English! Always the little yoke!

(*He laughs heartily.* BASIL *joins in half-heartedly.* Exit FELIX. BASIL'S *laughter subsides. He sits on the wicker seat* C., *facing* L. *Unseen by* BASIL, *a large fearsome man comes on at a steady trot from* U.R. *He wears fawn trousers taken in at the ankle, white rubber-soled canvas shoes and a bright red roll-collar sweater. This is* BRUCHIK. *He is a large, hairy man, having a beard and a mop of thick black hair, and he comes from an Eastern European Communist country.*)

He comes to R. *of the wicker seat* C. *and stands there.* BASIL *turns, reacts and cringes back on the wicker seat.*)

BASIL. Ooh!

BRUCHIK. Ve vill vin!

BASIL. I beg your pardon?

BRUCHIK. Ve—vill—vin!

BASIL. Oh—you will win? (BRUCHIK *nods.*) Yes, I'm sure you will.

BRUCHIK. Good-bye!

BASIL. Oh—good-bye.

(BRUCHIK *goes off* U.L. *at a trot.* BASIL *rises to the archway and gazes after him in horror.* NICOLETTE *returns from* R. *to the foot of the stairs.*)

BASIL. What was that?

NICOLETTE. What, monsieur?

BASIL. That—that *thing* that went through just now.

NICOLETTE. A man?

BASIL. Well, I don't know. It looked like a large red hedge. I suppose it must have been a man because it spoke to me.

NICOLETTE (*to* D.R.C.). He had a beard?

BASIL. Yes. I *think* you could say he had a beard.

NICOLETTE (*in to* C.). That is Monsieur Bruchik. He is staying here.

BASIL. In this hotel?

NICOLETTE. Yes. He is a runner.

BASIL. Well, I hope he keeps *on* running!

NICOLETTE. You have booked a room all right?

BASIL (*rapidly forgetting* BRUCHIK *and closing to* L. *of her with unconcealed admiration*). Yes, *very* all right, thank you.

NICOLETTE. Monsieur is here for ze games?

(*He looks at her.*)

BASIL. I beg your pardon?

NICOLETTE. Are you here for—ze games?

BASIL (*with a disarming smile*). I might be.

NICOLETTE. You do not know? (*Laughs and crosses below him to side table.*) Are you a good runner?

BASIL. I don't know. (*Towards her a pace, wolfishly.*) Are *you?*

NICOLETTE (*to table* D.L. *with three glasses*). Oh, I am not an athlete! (*Puts a glass on table* D.L.)

BASIL. Just a minute! What games are you talking about?

NICOLETTE. The Olympic Games!

BASIL. Oh, I thought you meant the *fun* and games.

NICOLETTE (*to* L. *of him*). The fun and games? What is that?
BASIL. Well, it's a sort of a—well, a kind of a—well, you know!
NICOLETTE (*to table* D.R.). So you are not here to take part in the Olympic Games? (*Put two glasses on table* D.R.)
BASIL (*easing* C.). No fear! I'm on holiday.
NICOLETTE. This is the first time we have had them here, so it is a great occasion for us. People are coming from all over the world. By tonight the hotels will be full and there will be no beds anywhere.
BASIL. It was lucky I arrived when I did. (*To* L. *of her*.) Are there any athletes staying here—apart from old Gorse Bush?
NICOLETTE (*going below him to side table* L.). Oh, yes! We have many already—and there are more to arrive.
BASIL (*a pace towards* C.). But I thought they all stayed together in a sort of Olympic Village?
NICOLETTE (*taking two glasses to above* L. *end of table* C.). That was the idea, but they found there was not enough room for all the athletes, so some of them are staying in hotels.
BASIL. I see.
NICOLETTE. Tonight we are expecting an English runner.
BASIL. Oh, who's that?
NICOLETTE. I think his name is Yo Smiss.
BASIL. You mean Joe Smith.
NICOLETTE. He should be arriving any moment now.

(MISS HACKET *comes down the stairs* R. *She is a wiry, bird-like little woman in her thirties, who seems to be continually on the move as she constantly limbers up. She comes across to* R. *of* BASIL. *She wears a blue track suit.*)

MISS HACKET. Any sign?
BASIL. I beg your pardon?
NICOLETTE (*to below* L. *end of table* C.) This is Monsieur—
BASIL. Trent. Basil Trent.
MISS HACKET. How do you do? My name's Hacket.
BASIL. Oh good!
MISS HACKET (*gently running on the spot*). I'm waiting for my baby.
BASIL. I see. Don't you think you ought to be sitting down?
MISS HACKET. I think you must have misunderstood me.
NICOLETTE. Miss Hacket is waiting for the English runner.
BASIL. Ah! Yo Smiss!
MISS HACKET (*she does knee-bending exercises, shaking her hands loosely.*

He unconsciously joins in). I've never met him before, so it's all rather exciting.
BASIL. Are you a relation?
MISS HACKET. Oh, no!
BASIL. Then—what exactly—?
MISS HACKET. I'm his trainer. His coach!
BASIL. But you're a woman. (*With a doubtful glance at her trousers.*) Aren't you?
MISS HACKET. That's right.
    (*He looks quizzically at* NICOLETTE, *and as he does so* MISS HACKET *squats down with bended knees and hands on hips. He looks back at her, finds she is not at eye-level, for a moment is unable to find her, then sees her and squats down beside her.*)
BASIL. That's very unusual.
MISS HACKET. I'm a very unusual woman.
    (*A car is heard arriving outside.*)
BASIL. So you're going to put him through his paces?
MISS HACKET. Correct! (*She rises violently, flinging her arms wide apart and catching him on the nose.*)
BASIL. Then why do you call him your baby?
MISS HACKET. I call them *all* my babies! I treat them like a mother, you see.
    (FELIX *comes rushing downstairs* R., *in great excitement.*)
FELIX. Nicolette! Nicolette! He is arriving! He is here!
NICOLETTE. The runner?
FELIX. Yes! He is outside now!
MISS HACKET. My baby!
FELIX (*crossing to the archway*). Come quickly! We must go and meet him! We must let him see that he is welcome!
MISS HACKET (*to* BASIL). He's here, you see.
BASIL. So I gathered.
MISS HACKET. I must go and meet him.
FELIX. Nicolette! Come on! Out to greet him!
NICOLETTE. Yes, Papa! I am coming!
    (MISS HACKET *and* NICOLETTE *rush out, followed by* FELIX, *calling the whole time.*
    BASIL *watches them go, slightly amazed. He shrugs and sits in the chair* L. *of table* C., *and lights a cigarette. As he does so we hear* FELIX'S *voice from outside.*)
FELIX (*off*). Bonjour! Bonjour! Bonjour! Welcome to L'Auberge

Blanche! We are honoured! We are thrilled! Bonjour! Bonjour! Bonjour!

(NICOLETTE *hurries on, carrying two suitcases, crosses below* BASIL *and puts them* D.R. *near the foot of the stairs. She then runs off again.* MISS HACKET *then runs on with a large suitcase held high above her head. She trots across, places it with the others, and then runs off again.* FELIX *staggers on with a heavy suitcase which he can hardly lift off the ground, places it* D.R. *and runs off again.*

BASIL *rises and as he does so* NICOLETTE, MISS HACKET *and* FELIX *return in that order with more parcels, etc.* BASIL *dodges out of their way and sits* L. *of table* D.L.)

FELIX. Here he comes! The English runner! He is here!

(FELIX, NICOLETTE *and* MISS HACKET *all stand* D.R. *facing the main entrance in great anticipation.* BASIL *shows only the mildest interest.*

HUMPHREY PODMORE *comes in through the archway. He is a meek little Yorkshireman, wearing a suit which is slightly too small for him, and a cloth cap. He carries a tiny attaché case, and rather incongruously smokes a cigar. He comes tentatively on to below the table* C., *and stands there rather shyly for a moment.*)

HUMPHREY. This is all most unexpected. I do hope I haven't put you to any trouble.

FELIX. But we are honoured! We are thrilled!

BASIL. Bonjour! Bonjour! Bonjour!

HUMPHREY. Oh, thank you. (*He casts a bewildered glance at* BASIL.) I wonder if you have a room?

FELIX. For you, m'sieur, we have the best room there is! We keep especially the best room for you!

HUMPHREY. I'm taken aback. Such consideration.

FELIX. For a person like yourself, representing your country in this fine way, for you nothing could be too good.

HUMPHREY. Representing my country? Well, that's very nice of you.

FELIX. We are honoured! We are thrilled!

NICOLETTE. You already said that, Papa.

FELIX. Be quiet, Nicolette.

HUMPHREY. I don't need anything very much. A little room will do.

FELIX. For you, m'sieur, the best room in the hotel! For you—the bridal chamber!

BASIL (*crossing eagerly to* L. *of* HUMPHREY *and shaking him by the hand*).

Well, congratulations! You're on your honeymoon! Isn't that nice? I wondered why you were wearing that hat.

HUMPHREY. Young man, I don't know who you are, but I'll have you know I'm not on my honeymoon!

BASIL. Really? And in the bridal chamber? What a waste!

FELIX. It is the best room in the hotel.

BASIL. I should jolly well hope so. (*Indicating the cases* D.R.) He hasn't brought his trousseau all this way for nothing.

HUMPHREY. I wanted something quiet and modest. I didn't expect such a reception.

FELIX. I understand, but only the best room is good enough for you. It has all been prepared.

HUMPHREY. You *knew* I was coming?

FELIX. Of course!

HUMPHREY. Oh, how very nice. I was lucky to get on a train, but there was a reserved seat unclaimed so they gave it to me. It was most lucky.

FELIX. Ah! the English sense of humour!

HUMPHREY. I wasn't trying to be funny.

FELIX. But you must surely have had the best reservation there was!

HUMPHREY. Oh, no. I told you, I didn't have one at all.

BASIL. I say, should you be smoking that thing?

HUMPHREY. What?

BASIL. It's awfully bad for the wind! (*Takes the cigar from him.*)

HUMPHREY. Now, look here, young man—!

MISS HACKET (*to* R. *of* HUMPHREY). He's quite right, baby.

HUMPHREY (*astounded*). *What* did you say?

MISS HACKET. You shouldn't be smoking it! It's very naughty.

HUMPHREY. But I *like* cigars! Give it back to me!

BASIL. Ah-ha! Don't snatch!

MISS HACKET. No, no, baby.

HUMPHREY. I don't wish to be rude, but I'm *not* your baby and will you please mind your own business!

MISS HACKET. I forbid it.

HUMPHREY. I beg your pardon?

MISS HACKET. It isn't allowed, don't you see?

HUMPHREY. Not allowed?

MISS HACKET. No.

HUMPHREY. Not ever?

MISS HACKET. No.

HUMPHREY. Why not?
BASIL. I told you, it's awfully bad for the wind!
HUMPHREY. Will you please go away!
FELIX (*to foot of stairs, anxious to avoid a scene*). Shall I show you to your room, m'sieur?
HUMPHREY. Yes, perhaps that would be a good idea. I think my case is over there somewhere.
FELIX. We will take them all to your room.
HUMPHREY. *All* of them?
FELIX. Of course.
HUMPHREY (*below* MISS HACKET *to* D.L. *of* NICOLETTE). But you can't do that.
FELIX. Monsieur, think nothing of it.
HUMPHREY. It's most unusual.
FELIX (*going up the stairs with some of the cases*). This way, m'sieur!
HUMPHREY (*to foot of stairs*). Thank you. Thank you.
FELIX. To the bridal chamber!
BASIL (*humming the "Wedding March"*). Da-da! Di-dum-da-da-da!
HUMPHREY (*going up the stairs, exasperated*). Ooh! Go to Halifax!
(*He goes off, preceded by* FELIX. BASIL *grins and smokes the cigar.* MISS HACKET *picks up some of the cases and goes off after the others.* NICOLETTE *looks rather sad.* BASIL *goes to* L. *of her.*)
BASIL. What's the matter?
NICOLETTE. Nothing.
BASIL. You look upset. Is anything wrong?
NICOLETTE. I am disappointed.
BASIL. What about?
NICOLETTE. That is the English runner?
BASIL. Er—yes. Yes, that's him.
NICOLETTE. He does not *look* like a runner.
BASIL. No, he doesn't, does he? Ah, but you wait till you see him in action!
NICOLETTE. I do not think I want to.
BASIL. I don't think *I* do either! (*Quickly.*) Oh, he'll be wonderful! All good runners look like that. What did you expect?
NICOLETTE (*wistfully*). Tall—big shoulders—little waist—and dark wavy hair!
BASIL. I see.
NICOLETTE. And what do I get? Short—*no* shoulders—big waist—and no hair at all!

BASIL. Well, it'll take a couple of days to get him into shape, you know.

NICOLETTE. A couple of days will do nothing.

(FELIX *appears at the top of the stairs.*)

FELIX. Nicolette! Come along! Bring some of these things.

NICOLETTE. Very good, Papa.

(She picks up some of the packages and goes off very reluctantly with FELIX.

BASIL *realizes that he does not really like cigars and quickly puts it out, pulling a wry face. He wanders across to look at the label on the remaining suitcase. As he bends to look at it,* AGNES PODMORE *comes on boisterously from* U.L. *and pounds on to* C.)

AGNES. Hey, you!

BASIL. What? (*He turns.*) Oh, hullo.

AGNES. Come here!

(*He crosses to her.*)

I'm looking for someone.

BASIL. Why? Are you in trouble?

AGNES. I'm looking for a man.

BASIL. Oh, just *looking* for trouble. Should he be here?

AGNES. No, he shouldn't! That's why I'm looking for him.

BASIL. What kind of a man is he?

AGNES. He's my husband.

BASIL. Oh, that kind of a man! What does he look like?

AGNES. Well, when he left me he was short, bald and respectable. Lord knows what he looks like now!

BASIL. Oh, he's left you?

AGNES. Of course he's left me!

BASIL. Of course!

AGNES. That's enough of that!

BASIL. Do you know his name?

AGNES. You fool! Of course I know his name. Humphrey Podmore. Have you seen him?

BASIL. No, I haven't.

AGNES (*moving* L.). I'd better look elsewhere.

BASIL. A very good idea.

AGNES (*turns abruptly to face him*). But—I shall be back!

BASIL. I'll tell him.

AGNES. What?

BASIL. I mean, if I *see* him, I'll tell him.

AGNES (*closing in to* L. *of* BASIL). You're not taking me for a ride, are you?
BASIL. Not likely!
AGNES. I'm not one to be played around with, you know.
BASIL. I can believe that.
AGNES. What did you say?
BASIL. Nothing at all.
AGNES. Well, you'll tell him that, won't you?
BASIL. What? Tell him nothing at all?
AGNES. No!—Tell him what I said.
BASIL. I expect he already knows.
AGNES. Knows what?
BASIL. That you're not one to be played around with.
AGNES. I didn't mean that!
BASIL. Oh, you *are* one to be played around with!
AGNES. I mean, tell him that I shall be back!
(FELIX *comes on from the stairs and goes to* R. *of* BASIL.)
FELIX. Ah! Bonjour! Bonjour! Bonjour! Welcome to L'Auberge Blanche. We are honoured.
BASIL. Never mind all that. She's not staying.
FELIX. But, madame, you must stay.
AGNES. Why?
BASIL. Yes, why?
FELIX. Because of the welcome we have for you.
AGNES. What welcome?
FELIX. The comfort, the hospitality, the wine, the food.
AGNES. I'm looking for a man.
FELIX. Well, that is a little unusual, but it could be arranged.
AGNES. Don't be disgusting!
FELIX. Oh, it is you again, madame! I did not recognize you at first.
AGNES (*to archway* U.L.). I shall look elsewhere. But remember!
AGNES
BASIL } (*together*). I shall be back!
(*Exit* AGNES U.L.)
FELIX. Did I misunderstand her, monsieur?
BASIL. Yes, I rather think you did, just a little.
FELIX. Ah! I am so sorry!
BASIL (*sitting* L. *of table* C.). That's all right. I'm delighted.
FELIX (*to* D.R. *of table* C.). You know that lady?
BASIL. I didn't. I do now.

FELIX. Who was this man, then, that she was looking for?
BASIL. Oh, nobody you know.
FELIX (to archway U.L.). I must catch her up and apologize. Then perhaps she will stay at my hotel.
BASIL. Do you very much *want* her to stay at your hotel?
FELIX. Monsieur, if you are a fisherman you wish to catch fish—yes?
BASIL. Yes.
FELIX. I am a hotel-keeper—so I catch her up and apologise!
  (*Exit* FELIX U.L. HUMPHREY *comes on from* R. *He has taken off his hat*.)
BASIL. Well, settled in nice and cosily?
HUMPHREY. I don't know that I'm speaking to you. You were very rude to me. (*Moves away up to* L. *of table* U.R.)
BASIL. I'm sorry. I didn't mean to be. Come and have a drink.
HUMPHREY. No, thank you.
BASIL. Of course. I forgot. You're in training. Well, do sit down.
  (HUMPHREY *sits tentatively on wicker seat above table* C.)
There! That's better. My name is Basil Trent.
HUMPHREY. How do you do? My name is Podmore.
BASIL. What?
HUMPHREY. Humphrey Podmore. (BASIL *laughs and* HUMPHREY *rises*.) Now, look here—!
BASIL. I'm sorry. It's just that I'd heard the name before somewhere. Quite recently, in fact. I wonder where it was? (HUMPHREY *sits again*.) Is your room all right?
HUMPHREY. Yes, thank you. I've got a balcony.
BASIL. I'm *so* glad!
HUMPHREY. But they insisted on bringing all that luggage into my room. I did try to stop them.
BASIL. It *is* the usual place for luggage to go, in your room.
HUMPHREY. Yes. But, you see it isn't mine.
BASIL. Not yours?
HUMPHREY. Oh, no. I only brought one suitcase with me.
BASIL. Then who *does* it belong to?
HUMPHREY. I've no idea.
BASIL. You know, you're liable to get into trouble taking somebody else's luggage.
HUMPHREY. I didn't take it!
BASIL. We've only your word for that. It's in your room, isn't it? That's bound to look suspicious.

HUMPHREY. I tell you, I didn't take it!
BASIL. When the police come you're going to look pretty guilty with a room full of stolen luggage.
HUMPHREY. But I can explain!
BASIL. All right! How did it get there? Explain that.
HUMPHREY (*lamely*). I don't know.
BASIL. There! You see! Guilty as hell. (*Takes out a cigarette.*)
HUMPHREY. Presumably it was addressed here.
BASIL. Has it got your name on it?
HUMPHREY. Of course not!
BASIL. And yet it's in your room. You'll have a lot of explaining to do in the morning. (*Gets out lighter.*) What did you say?
HUMPHREY. Nothing.
BASIL. That's good. (*Works lighter.*) Are you *going* to say anything?
HUMPHREY. No.
BASIL. That's even better. (*Lights cigarette.*) You don't have to stop breathing, you know.
HUMPHREY (*pathetically*). And all I wanted was a quiet holiday.
BASIL. Quiet holiday? You chose a good place for that.
HUMPHREY. And I must say they've all behaved in the most charming manner.
BASIL. Well, it's a great honour for them to have you staying here.
HUMPHREY. That's what they keep telling me. And yet, in England, nobody cares tuppence about the Little Bruddersford Fruiterers' and Greengrocers' Association.
     (BASIL *looks at him.*)
BASIL. I beg your pardon?
HUMPHREY. I said nobody cares tuppence about the Little Bruddersford Fruiterers' and Greengrocers' Association.
BASIL. That's what I thought you said. All this is just a side-line, then?
HUMPHREY. All what?
BASIL. Well—running, athletics, the Olympic Games!
HUMPHREY. Good heavens, *I'm* not a runner.
BASIL. Are you sure?
HUMPHREY. Young man, do you think I'm drunk? I know if I'm a runner or not.
BASIL. Perhaps you'll have a drink then?
   (NICOLETTE *comes on from* R., *and is crossing to* L., *carefully avoiding looking at* HUMPHREY. *She gets to* L. *of* BASIL.)
Ah! Nicolette!

NICOLETTE. Yes, Mister Basil?
BASIL (*to* HUMPHREY). There, isn't that nice? Mister Basil! You stay here for a few days and she may call you "Mister Humphrey". Two large whiskies, please, Nicolette.
NICOLETTE (*with a look towards* HUMPHREY). Two?
BASIL. Er—yes. I'm a bit thirsty.
NICOLETTE. Very well. I will get them.
    (*With a painful look in the direction of* HUMPHREY, *she goes off* L.C.)
BASIL. So you're here under false pretences?
HUMPHREY. No, I am not!
BASIL. Your crimes are mounting up! First of all you steal some luggage, then you pretend to be someone else. Are you on the run?
HUMPHREY. Certainly not!
BASIL. Well, at this rate you jolly soon will be!
HUMPHREY. I can explain.
BASIL (*resuming his seat*). Well, come on, then.
    (*Pause.* HUMPHREY *moves up to* L. *end of wicker seat.*)
HUMPHREY. Can you keep a secret?
BASIL. I can try.
HUMPHREY. I *am* on the run.
BASIL. From the police?
HUMPHREY. No. From my wife.
BASIL (*suddenly*). Of course! Humphrey Podmore!
HUMPHREY. What's the matter?
BASIL. Oh, nothing. Just something I remembered. Why did you do it?
HUMPHREY. My wife has become a very difficult woman lately.
BASIL. I can believe that!
HUMPHREY. I warned her many times, but one day she went too far.
BASIL. Really? What did she do?
HUMPHREY. She called me a nincompoop!
BASIL. A nincompoop? Good heavens!
HUMPHREY. So I packed my bag and walked out.
BASIL. Well done!
HUMPHREY. You won't tell anyone?
BASIL. No, of course not. But you haven't been very clever, you know. You should have used an alias. Called yourself Smith or something.
HUMPHREY. I never thought of that.

BASIL. You *have* got a lot to learn!
　　(NICOLETTE *enters with two drinks. She goes above* BASIL *to between them.*)
HUMPHREY. So from now on I'm kicking over the traces! My bonnet's over the windmill! And I shall start tonight—at the Casino!
　　(NICOLETTE *puts down their drinks on the table.* HUMPHREY, *in a fit of enthusiasm, grabs her by the waist and pulls her on to his knee.*)
Oh, this is really living!
　　(NICOLETTE *pulls herself away from him, and goes off with obvious annoyance.*)
BASIL. Down the hatch!
HUMPHREY. Cheers!
　　(*They both drink. There is a pause.* HUMPHREY *giggles thoughtfully.*)
I wonder what Agnes would say if she could see me now!
BASIL. You may soon find out.
HUMPHREY. Eh?
BASIL. She's here.
HUMPHREY. What?
BASIL. Your wife. She's here.
HUMPHREY. Impossible!
BASIL. Someone's been looking for you.
HUMPHREY. For me?
BASIL. That's right. A woman.
HUMPHREY. Oh! Not a *large* woman?
BASIL. Very large.
HUMPHREY. And a loud woman?
BASIL. Yes.
HUMPHREY. How loud?
BASIL. Very loud.
HUMPHREY. Oh, lord! (*He rises.*) What did you say to her?
BASIL. I said I hadn't seen you.
HUMPHREY. Where did she go?
BASIL. She went elsewhere. But she said she'd be back.
HUMPHREY. When?
BASIL. She didn't say. I imagine fairly soon.
HUMPHREY (*away to* D.R. *of table* C.). Oh, what misfortune!
BASIL. You'll have to lie low until she's passed on.
　　(FELIX *returns from* U.L., *a trifle breathless.*)
FELIX. I'm afraid she misunderstood me.

BASIL. Why? What did you say?
FELIX. I said I would like to see her sleep in one of my rooms.
BASIL. Let that be a lesson to you. (*To* HUMPHREY.) He tried to bring her back.
HUMPHREY. Oh, thank heaven you failed!
FELIX. She is your wife, m'sieur?
HUMPHREY. I'm afraid so.
FELIX. Why did you bring her to Europe with you?
HUMPHREY. I didn't bring her. She came of her own accord.
FELIX. Couldn't trust you, eh, m'sieur? Ah! I can understand you not wanting to see her. She is a strong woman!
           (*He goes off,* L.C., *holding his cheek.*)
HUMPHREY (*to above table* C.). What am I going to do? She's bound to come back.
BASIL. You'll have to hide.
HUMPHREY. But where?
BASIL. I don't know. Anywhere that's convenient.
           (MISS HACKET *comes on from upstairs. She trots across to* R. *of their table.*)
MISS HACKET. I'm Hacket.
HUMPHREY. Oh?
MISS HACKET. They told you all about me, of course?
HUMPHREY. No, I don't—
BASIL (*quickly*). Yes, of course they did! You remember!
HUMPHREY. Do I?
BASIL. Miss Hacket. (*Nudges* HUMPHREY.)
HUMPHREY. Oh, yes—of course.
MISS HACKET. Pulse, please.
HUMPHREY. H'm?
           (*She grabs hold of his wrist and starts counting.*)
  Now, look here—!
MISS HACKET. S'sh! (*Finishes counting to herself.*) All right!
           (*She sees* HUMPHREY'S *glass and picks it up. She sniffs at it.*)
MISS HACKET. Tut! tut! tut! You naughty boy! None of that!
           (*She empties the whisky into a flower pot.*)
HUMPHREY. What do you think you're—
MISS HACKET. Don't let me catch you doing that again!
           (*She puts the empty glass on the table* D.R. *and runs off again up the stairs.*)
HUMPHREY. What on earth—

BASIL. Now, now! Calm down!

HUMPHREY. What did she think she was doing?

BASIL (*gaily*). She's quite right. It's awfully bad for your wind. (*Puts his feet up on the table.*)

HUMPHREY. Oh, bother my wind! And anyhow, what's my wind got to do with her?

BASIL (*sipping his whisky*). Well, she *is* your trainer.

HUMPHREY. My what?

BASIL. Your trainer. You seem to forget that you're here for the Olympic Games.

HUMPHREY. But I've explained all that to you.

BASIL. You haven't explained it to them.

HUMPHREY. But I'm *not* here for the Olympic Games!

BASIL. Then what *are* you here for?

HUMPHREY. I'm here for the—the—

BASIL. The *other* games!

HUMPHREY (*away to* L. *of table* D.R.). No, no, no!

BASIL. Well, if you're not here for the Olympic Games, and you're not here for the other games, I can't think why you didn't stay in England!

HUMPHREY (*turning*). But I've told you why! What are you up to? I told you I came here to get away from my wife.

BASIL. You don't seem to have succeeded. She's probably prowling about outside at this moment.

(FELIX *comes on from* L.C. *to below table* C. *He is followed by a reluctant* NICOLETTE. *He carries a small box camera.* NICOLETTE *hovers at the entrance* L.C.)

FELIX. Excuse me, please, gentlemen.

BASIL. Yes, of course.

FELIX. Come along, Nicolette. (*She moves to* D.L. *of him. To* HUMPHREY.) Please, it is a great honour to have you stay with us, m'sieur. We are delighted!

FELIX
BASIL } (*together*). We are thrilled!

BASIL. Bonjour! Bonjour! Bonjour! Oh, I beg your pardon.

FELIX. This is my daughter, Nicolette. Alas! my wife is not with us.

BASIL. Oh. I'm terribly sorry. (*Looks solemn.*)

FELIX. No, she is staying with her sister in Alsace.

BASIL. Oh, I see.

FELIX. And so she will not be here for the great event on Friday.

HUMPHREY. What great event?

(BASIL *to* L. *of* HUMPHREY.)

FELIX. Your race, m'sieur. (*With tremendous effect.*) The five thousand metres.

HUMPHREY (*in a whisper to* BASIL). Five thousand what?

BASIL (*whispering also*). You heard him—metres.

HUMPHREY (*whispering*). Five thousand of them?

FELIX. But of course.

HUMPHREY (*loudly to* FELIX). On Friday?

BASIL (*as* FELIX *looks puzzled*). He always gets a bit muddled over days. (*Business with* HUMPHREY.)

FELIX. Oh, you English! You always muddle through! And yet you always win in the end. Anyway, my wife—Nicolette's mother—

BASIL. Oh, she's Nicolette's mother, too! (*As he gets a glare from* FELIX.) Sorry.

FELIX. She will not be here to see you run on Friday, so I thought it would be nice to send her a photosnap of you. (*Puts an arm around* NICOLETTE.) Perhaps with my daughter, Nicolette. (*She breaks away to table* D.L.) It would be a great honour.

HUMPHREY (*going below* BASIL *to* C.). Well, as a matter of fact, there's something I have to explain.

BASIL (*grabbing* HUMPHREY'S *right arm*). He'd be delighted! Wouldn't you?

HUMPHREY. Well, I—

BASIL. There! You see! What about just over here, eh? (*Pushes* HUMPHREY *into position* R. *of table* C.)

FELIX (*to* R. *of* NICOLETTE). Now, come on, Nicolette. I want you to be in the picture, too.

NICOLETTE. Do I *have* to, Papa?

FELIX (*sotto voce*). Of course! Come on!

NICOLETTE. I do not want to.

FELIX. Do as you are told.

(FELIX *pushes her and she goes and stands* L. *of* HUMPHREY, *and they pose very unnaturally.* BASIL *sits in chair* L. *of table* D.R.)

BASIL. There! Isn't that lovely? So natural!

FELIX (*in to* D.L. *of* NICOLETTE). One moment, m'sieur.

HUMPHREY. Yes?

FELIX. May I ask one more favour?

HUMPHREY. I suppose so. But you're making a great mistake.

FELIX. You are famous for your running, so please—might we just see a little piece of your legs?
(HUMPHREY *reacts*. BASIL *laughs*.)
HUMPHREY. Well, that's most irregular.
FELIX. Irregular to see a runner's legs?
HUMPHREY. No, no, but—
BASIL. Perhaps he means his *legs* are irregular.
HUMPHREY. Nothing of the sort!
BASIL. *Are* your legs irregular?
HUMPHREY. Certainly not!
BASIL. All right, then—let's see them!
HUMPHREY. I don't care for all this nudity.
FELIX (*resuming his place to take the photograph*). Please, monsieur, just a little bit of leg for the photosnap.
BASIL. Come on, you heard him! A little bit of leg for the photosnap.
(*Very reluctantly, and with great embarrassment,* HUMPHREY *pulls up his trousers to below the knee.* FELIX *takes the photograph.*)
FELIX. Thank you! Thank you so much! Come, Nicolette! Mamma will be so pleased!
(*Exit* FELIX L.C., *followed by* NICOLETTE. HUMPHREY *starts to re-arrange his trousers facing* BASIL, *then turns his back to* BASIL *to do so.*)
HUMPHREY. Why wouldn't you let me tell them the truth?
BASIL (*evasively, moving* U.S.). It would have upset them. You don't want to spoil their fun, do you?
HUMPHREY (*following up to* R. *of* BASIL). The truth never upset anyone!
BASIL (*to* U.C.). Apart from anything else, they would have been very angry.
HUMPHREY. Why?
BASIL (*turning to face him*). Well, you *did* lead them up the garden path, didn't you?
HUMPHREY. How?
BASIL. You said you were an Olympic runner.
HUMPHREY (*up level with* BASIL). I did not! They *assumed* that I was!
BASIL. You didn't deny it.
HUMPHREY. I was greeted at the station. They seemed to know which seat I was travelling in. I thought they must have heard about my work in England. I was touched by their attention.
BASIL. And so you allowed yourself to be driven here, acclaimed like

royalty and given the best room in the hotel! If they'd known you were only a greenfly on the Little Bruddersford Fruiterers' and Greengrocers' Association, you wouldn't have even got a camp bed out in the garden! (*Moves* U.S. *to look over balustrade* U.C.)

HUMPHREY (*up to* R. *of* BASIL). At the station they spoke a foreign language.

BASIL. What did you expect? They're foreigners!

HUMPHREY. I mean that was why I misunderstood their intentions. (*Breaking slightly* R.) I'll have to explain the whole situation to them.

BASIL (*turning suddenly after a pause*). I say!

HUMPHREY. Yes?

BASIL. A thought has struck me. Where is the *real* runner they were expecting?

HUMPHREY. I don't know. I suppose the reservation I got on the train was intended for him. For some reason he didn't turn up. I only wish he was here now.

BASIL (*to* L. *of* HUMPHREY). But he isn't.

HUMPHREY. He very soon will be. I'm going while the going is good! (*Starts to go* R.)

BASIL. Oh, no, you're not.

HUMPHREY (*stopping and turning*). What do you mean?

BASIL. I've got an idea.

HUMPHREY (*to.* R. *of* BASIL). Oh, no! Please! I've got to go!

BASIL (*down to above chair* L. *of table* C.). Supposing the real runner doesn't turn up in time for the race on Friday?

HUMPHREY. I don't care! I've got to go!

BASIL. What? And dear old England have one less representative in the five thousand metres? Where's your patriotism?

HUMPHREY (*unconsciously coming to attention*). Now you're striking below the belt!

BASIL (*sitting chair* L. *of table* C.). We couldn't let the old country down, could we? And disappoint all the people here? They expect to see you running on Friday.

HUMPHREY (D.S. *a little*). Not me! *Him!*

BASIL. But *he* isn't here.

HUMPHREY (*facing away* R.). Oh no, no, no! Emphatically no! I refuse to be made a laughing stock!

BASIL (*sadly*). All right, Humphrey. If you want to let the old country down. But there are—chaps back home—relying on you.

HUMPHREY. Not me! *Him!*

BASIL. Relying on you to—to keep the old flag flying. (*He appears to be very moved.*)
HUMPHREY. Fiddlesticks! You're up to something and I don't know what it is. I refuse to deceive these people a moment longer. I shall tell them the truth and apologize. (*He goes above* BASIL'S *chair to* L. *of it.*)
BASIL. Perhaps I'd better tell the police about that luggage in your room, after all.

(HUMPHREY *turns and glares at him as* FELIX *enters* L.C. *in a hurry.*)

FELIX. Monsieur! She is here again!
BASIL. Who?
FELIX. The lady with the heavy hand.
HUMPHREY. My wife!
FELIX. Yes, m'sieur!
BASIL. Oh, good!
HUMPHREY. You'll have to hide me somewhere.
FELIX. This way, monsieur!

(HUMPHREY *rushes across to* R. *of* FELIX, *then turns to face* BASIL.)

HUMPHREY. Get rid of her for me, will you?
BASIL. Well, that rather depends.
HUMPHREY. What do you mean by that?
BASIL. It would be very easy for me to send her away. And then again, it would be just as easy for me to tell her you were here.
HUMPHREY (*returning a pace*). You wouldn't do that?
BASIL. I might.
HUMPHREY (*to* L. *of* BASIL'S *chair*). Oh, no! You couldn't!
BASIL. Well, you see, unless I'm sure you agree to what I suggested just now, I might forget myself and tell her.
HUMPHREY. This is blackmail!
BASIL. Oh, is it? What fun! I've always wanted to do a bit of quiet blackmail.
FELIX (*he goes to look through archway*). Hurry, monsieur! She will be here at any moment!
BASIL. You haven't much time to decide.
FELIX. Whatever it is, please decide quickly!
HUMPHREY. Oh, very well, I agree! Provided you get rid of her.
BASIL. Good! Remember now—you've made a promise!
HUMPHREY. Oh, cat among the pigeons!

(*Exit* HUMPHREY L.C., *followed by* FELIX. BASIL *rises and moves below the table* C. *to* D.R. *of it. A second later* AGNES *pounds on from* U.L. *to* D.L. *of table* C.)

BASIL. Ah! Back again?

AGNES. I *said* I was coming back.

BASIL. So you did.

AGNES. I'm a woman of my word.

BASIL. Yes, I bet you are.

AGNES. Any sign?

BASIL. I beg your pardon?

AGNES. Any sign? Any sign?

BASIL. Not a thing! Not a thing!

AGNES. Has anybody arrived?

BASIL. Yes.

AGNES. Who?

BASIL. You and me.

AGNES. Since I *left!*

BASIL. Oh—only you.

AGNES. Don't be a fool, man! (*She sees the empty whisky glass on table* C.) Whose glass is this?

BASIL. Mine.

AGNES. And the one over there? (*Indicating the one on the table* D.R.)

BASIL. Oh, well, yes, somebody *did* arrive.

AGNES. What was his name?

BASIL. Yo Smiss.

AGNES. What?

BASIL. He's a runner.

AGNES. Then why is he drinking?

BASIL. It's only medicinal.

AGNES. Medicinal! What's wrong with him?

BASIL. It's his back.

AGNES. *Back?*

BASIL. Very bad back.

AGNES. Very bad back?

BASIL. Yes. Catches him just here.

AGNES. And he's running in the Olympic Games?

BASIL. On Friday.

AGNES. With a bad back?

BASIL. A *very* bad back.

AGNES. That'll be an interesting race.

BASIL. You can say that again!
(*Enter* MISS HACKET *down the stairs.*)
MISS HACKET. Where is he? The naughty boy!
BASIL. Oh, he's gone inside.
MISS HACKET. I'll find him. (*Moves to* R. *of* BASIL.)
BASIL (*dropping down to intercept her*). No, not that way. *That* way. (*Indicates stairs.*)
MISS HACKET. Don't be silly. I just came out that way. I would have seen him. I'll have a look in here.
(*She goes below* BASIL *to* L. *of him.*)
BASIL. But he's not there, I assure you! I expect you missed him. He went up to his room.
MISS HACKET. I've just come from there.
BASIL. Oh, so you have. Well, he's definitely not that way. I'd have another look up there if I were you.
MISS HACKET. No. I think I'll find him over here. (*She starts to go, and gets to* D.L. *of* AGNES.)
BASIL. Why do you want him now? Couldn't it wait?
MISS HACKET. It could not. I've got to get him into some sort of shape by Friday.
BASIL. Well—er—could you give a sort of a whistle before you come out?
MISS HACKET. Whatever for?
BASIL. Well, I—I thought it would be a nice gesture.
MISS HACKET. To what?
BASIL (*thinking hard*). Well, you see—he used to be in the Navy—and he likes to be piped everywhere.
MISS HACKET. Oh, does he?
BASIL. So if you could give just a few trills before you brought him out it would—well, remind him of the old days.
MISS HACKET. I'm afraid I can't whistle. And, anyhow, I thought you said I wouldn't find him over here? (*Exit* L.)
AGNES. I think I'll be going.
BASIL. A good idea!
AGNES. On second thoughts I'd like some tea. (*Sits* L. *of table* C.)
BASIL. *Not* such a good idea. (*To* R. *of table* C.) I wouldn't recommend it. It's not very good.
AGNES. Then I'll have some wine.
BASIL. Have you brought a glass with you?
AGNES. A glass? Of course not.

BASIL. Then you can't have any wine.
AGNES. They provide glasses here.
BASIL. Oh, no!
AGNES. I tell you they do! This is an hotel! Do you think I'm mad?
BASIL. It's a new rule here. There were so many breakages last year. Breakages—and thefts! So from now on, the rule is "No glass, no wine".
AGNES. Don't be ridiculous! I shall wait here until I see the manager.

(FELIX *comes on* L.C. *He signals wildly to* BASIL. AGNES *turns and sees him.* FELIX *goes off in confusion.*)

BASIL (*in explanation*). An old school friend of mine.
AGNES. He's the manager here.
BASIL. Yes. It was a very good school. Don't you just love this part of Europe? The dances here are exquisite!
AGNES. Oh, are they?
BASIL. Yes. Haven't you seen them dancing in the streets? Oh, they're very good! They sort of clap their hands and stamp their feet and everything all at the same time—rather like this! (*He demonstrates.*)
AGNES. Are you mad?
BASIL. Shall we dance?
AGNES. Let me go! Let me go!

(BASIL *grabs the horrified* AGNES *in his arms and proceeds to pull her around in a wild dance, being careful to keep her face pressed into his bosom, as* MISS HACKET *comes on pushing a protesting* HUMPHREY *in front of her.*

BASIL *succeeds in keeping* AGNES'S *face hidden as* HUMPHREY *and* MISS HACKET *go quickly across the stage and off* R. BASIL *stops dancing and releases* AGNES *who sits* L. *of table* C. *He is now* L. *of her chair.*)

AGNES. Well, *really!*
BASIL. You dance divinely.
AGNES. You're a scoundrel!
BASIL. And *you're* as light as a feather!
AGNES (*rising*). I'm going now. But you needn't think you've heard the last of this because you haven't! There's more going on here than meets the eye! (*Turning in the archway.*) And remember—
BASIL
AGNES } (*together*). I shall be back!
AGNES. Ooh!

(*Exit* AGNES U.L. FELIX *comes on with* NICOLETTE, L.C.)

FELIX. Did she see him?

BASIL. I don't think so. Anyway, she's gone now.
FELIX. It is such a pity she has to come with him. How can he concentrate on his running when *she* is around?
BASIL. Oh, I dunno. It might encourage him.
FELIX. Please, how is her name "Podmore" when his name is "Joe Smith"? That I do not understand.
BASIL. Well, he's travelling incognito, you see.
FELIX. Ah! (*But he does not understand.*) Thank you so much. We must make sure that she does not return again.

(*Exit* FELIX L.C. NICOLETTE *collects the dirty whisky glass from table* C.)

NICOLETTE. Your wife has not yet come, Mister Basil.
BASIL (*to* L. *of chair* L. *of table* C.). What wife? Oh, *my* wife! Oh, yes. No, she hasn't, has she?
NICOLETTE. Do you know when she is coming?
BASIL. No idea!
NICOLETTE. What is she like?
BASIL. Oh, she's—she's sort of—er—well, you know.
NICOLETTE. She is dark?
BASIL. Sometimes. I mean—in some lights she's dark, and in other lights, she's fair. It depends.
NICOLETTE (*she crosses to the table* D.R. *and collects the other dirty glass*). I do not think you tell the truth. I do not think you have got a wife at all.
BASIL (*to below table* C.). You don't?
NICOLETTE. No. I think you make that up.
BASIL. Do you?
NICOLETTE. You order a double bedroom but you have no wife. That is rather sad.
BASIL (*to* D.R.C.). Well, I like to be prepared. I mean, I might *get* married. You never know.
NICOLETTE. I think you are a naughty man.
BASIL. Do you?
NICOLETTE. I think so! (*She giggles saucily.*)
BASIL (*with a grin*). Not a word to father about this, eh?
NICOLETTE (*smiles, shakes her head*). Not a word.
BASIL. A wife may turn up, you never know.
NICOLETTE (*laughing*). Oooh! I think you are a *very* naughty man!

(*A beautiful young lady wanders in from* U.L. *She wears a light summer coat over a dress, and carries a travelling case and a handbag.*

Her name is PAULINE MARYOT. *She comes to below the* R. *end of table* C.)

BASIL (*to* NICOLETTE). What did I tell you!

(BASIL *crosses to* R. *of* PAULINE *and beams at her.* NICOLETTE *watches him reproachfully.*)

BASIL. Ah! Welcome to L'Auberge Blanche! We are honoured! We are thrilled! Bonjour! Bonjour! Bonjour!

PAULINE. Good afternoon.

BASIL (*closing in very near to her*). Yes, it is! A *very* good afternoon!

(*He gazes at her admiringly. She is slightly embarrassed.*)

PAULINE. I should like a room.

BASIL. Of course you would.

NICOLETTE. We are full up!

PAULINE. Oh, but I—

BASIL. Full up? Don't pay any attention to the child! I'm sure we can squeeze you in somewhere.

NICOLETTE (*in a pace*). There are no rooms left.

BASIL. Of course there are. Get me the register.

NICOLETTE. I will not! I will get my father! (*She goes off,* L.C., *crossly.*)

BASIL. These youngsters don't understand. (*To* L. *to collect the register.*) Now, what sort of a room had you in mind? (*Returning to* L. *of her.*)

PAULINE. Oh, I don't know.

BASIL. A single room, of course?

PAULINE. Yes.

BASIL. Good!

PAULINE. Are you the manager?

BASIL. Er—well, not exactly, no.

PAULINE. What do you mean, not exactly?

BASIL. Well, I mean—you see, I—(*He smiles broadly.*) No. I'm *not* the manager.

PAULINE. I thought not, somehow. You don't look like a manager.

BASIL. Oh. What *do* I look like?

NICOLETTE (*entering at this moment*). A naughty man!

BASIL. Go away!

(FELIX *follows* NICOLETTE *on and gets to* D.L. *of* BASIL. NICOLETTE *to* D.L.)

FELIX. Ah! Welcome to L'Auberge Blanche! We are—

BASIL. It's all right. I did all that.

FELIX. I would very much like to welcome you to my hotel, but, of course, we are very full at this time.
PAULINE. But I have a reservation.
FELIX. Oh, that is different.
PAULINE. My name is Pauline Maryot.
BASIL. Of course it is! How could it be anything else but—Pauline Maryot! (*Looking in the register.*) Here you are. It's in the register. Room twenty-four. That's right next to me. I'm room twenty-five.
NICOLETTE. The odd numbers are on the other side.
BASIL (*without taking his eyes off* PAULINE). That can be changed.
PAULINE. I believe you have an English runner staying with you?
BASIL. English runner?
PAULINE. I said I would meet him here.
BASIL. You'd *meet* him? *Here?*
PAULINE. Yes.
BASIL. You mean—you mean you *know* him?
PAULINE. Yes, of course.
FELIX. Oh, he will be very pleased!
BASIL. I'm not so sure. How—how well do you know him?
PAULINE. *Very* well. Of course I haven't seen him for about a year, but I don't expect he's changed much in that time.
BASIL. You'd be surprised!
PAULINE. He's arrived, then?
BASIL. Oh, yes. He's here. Look, Nicolette, why don't you go and find the gentleman?
FELIX (*to* NICOLETTE). Yes. Go and tell him the good news!
NICOLETTE (*crossing to* R.). All right, Papa. I will go.
BASIL (*as she goes*). Tell him there's somebody down here who knows him—somebody who knows him very well—in case he's thinking of coming down.

   (NICOLETTE *goes off* R. BASIL *mops his brow.* AGNES *returns at speed and comes to* C.)

(*Calling after* NICOLETTE.) Make that two!
AGNES. I wish to book a room at this hotel.
MISS HACKET (*off*). Come along, baby! Get those knees up!

   (*The ladies look towards the stairs* R. BASIL *and* FELIX *panic.* BASIL *pushes* AGNES, *who knocks into* FELIX. *He sits abruptly in the chair at table* D.L. *with* AGNES *on his lap.*)

BASIL (*to* PAULINE). Darling!

(*He grabs* PAULINE *and kisses her firmly. And at that moment* HUMPHREY *runs down the stairs in running shorts, vest and tennis shoes. He is followed by* MISS HACKET, *calling the whole time.* NICOLETTE *returns and remains at the top of the stairs.*)

MISS HACKET. One—two—three—four! One—two—three—four!

(AGNES *slaps* FELIX'S *face.* PAULINE *slaps* BASIL'S *face.* HUMPHREY *and* MISS HACKET *run off through the archway* U.L.)

QUICK CURTAIN

ACT TWO

The next morning. It is a bright, sunny day.

NICOLETTE *is laying the tables for breakfast, singing as she does so. As the curtain rises, she moves up from the table* D.R. *to above the* C. *table and proceeds to lay it for two.*

FELIX *comes on from* L.C. NICOLETTE *looks up from her work, sees that he has got a black eye and laughs.*

FELIX. What is the matter?
NICOLETTE. Your eye, Papa!
FELIX (*seriously*). Oh, yes, it is very funny.
NICOLETTE. Did the lady do that to you?
FELIX. Yes. The well-built lady.
NICOLETTE. Let that be a lesson to you!
FELIX. What do you mean?
NICOLETTE. You shouldn't have pulled her on to your knee.
FELIX. I did not pull her! She was pushed! My knee just happened to be there.
NICOLETTE. I do not think that Mamma would believe that.
FELIX (*to* L. *of table* C.). It is the truth! I was standing up. Mr. Basil push the lady—she push into me—so I sit down.
NICOLETTE. H'm?
FELIX. She is a very *big* lady! I sit down, and so my lap is there, and so she sit in it. It was terrible!
NICOLETTE. Where has the big lady gone to now?
FELIX. I do not know. I think she must be staying at the big hotel down the road. She disappeared, and I for one was very relieved. I do not want her to stay in my hotel.
NICOLETTE. But, Papa, if you want the hotel to be full you must have everybody staying here.
FELIX. You are right, Nicolette. (*Shrugs and moves to* D.R. *of table* C.) But even if the hotel is always full it will not help if I cannot pay the money I owe. I have only a little savings. It is not enough.
NICOLETTE (*easing slightly* L.). Is there anything we can do?
FELIX. We can only hope that something good will turn up.

(*Enter* BASIL *from the stairs. He is now dressed in a gay shirt, slacks, and sandals.*)

BASIL. Well, here I am!

(*As* BASIL *turns we see that he also has a black eye. They meet* D.R.C.)

BASIL }
FELIX } (*together*). Oh, look at your eye!

(*They link fingers.*)

FELIX. Shakespeare.

BASIL. Freeman, Hardy and Willis.

NICOLETTE (*dropping down* L.C.). You did not do so well with the lady.

BASIL (*to* C.). Oh, this! That was only a minor skirmish. There's plenty of time.

NICOLETTE. I do not wish to know that. (*Away to the side table where she collects crockery and goes to table* D.L.)

BASIL. Oh, very well. You brought it up.

FELIX. M'sieur, my eye is blacker than yours.

BASIL. Well, your lady was bigger than mine.

FELIX. Yes, indeed!

BASIL. Where is she now?

FELIX. Gone.

BASIL. For good?

FELIX. I should not think so.

BASIL. Neither should I!

FELIX. How is your friend this morning?

BASIL. Oh, he's—he's all right. I think.

FELIX. Have you not seen him?

BASIL. Not actually. I went in to see him and he threw something at me.

FELIX. Why was he so angry?

BASIL. I think I disturbed his slumber. He's feeling pretty stiff this morning.

FELIX. Stiff?

BASIL. After the running he did last night.

FELIX. Will he be all right for the race?

BASIL. I hope so!

FELIX. What?

BASIL. I said I should hope so. I mean, he's been practising for months for this, you know. He's in pretty tip-top condition.

FELIX. Then why is he so stiff?

BASIL. Oh—the reaction. You know, the new surroundings, change of climate and all that. It always affects him. (*To* L. *of* FELIX.) By the way, do you know a bookie?
FELIX. A—bookie? What is this?
BASIL. Oh—you know! A man who takes bets.
FELIX. Ach, so! Yes. I know. You wish to place a bet?
BASIL. Yes, please. (*Takes out a bulky envelope and hands it to* FELIX.) Here's the money. I've put the details inside.
FELIX. It is for on the race that your friend is running in?
BASIL. Yes, that's right. Can you get it on for me right away?
FELIX. Yes. It feels like a lot of money.
BASIL. It's a pony.
FELIX (*amazed*). A pony? In *here?*
BASIL. Yes.
FELIX. But a pony—that is a little horse.
BASIL. Oh, no! A pony is twenty-five pounds.
FELIX. You put twenty-five pounds on your friend's race?
BASIL. Yes.
FELIX. It is a lot of money to gamble.
BASIL. This isn't a gamble. It's a ruddy certainty.
FELIX. You are so sure of the result?
BASIL. Oh, there's no doubt where *he'll* come in!
FELIX (*in a daze*). I will take it to him now. (*He crosses below* BASIL *to* L.C.)
BASIL. Good show!
FELIX. Nicolette, you look after everything here until I return.
NICOLETTE. Yes, Papa.
FELIX (*going*). Twenty-five pounds. (*Turning.*) How much will you make if your friend wins?
BASIL (*taken off guard*). If he *wins?* (*Quickly.*) Oh, if he wins—oh—er —oh, quite a lot.
FELIX. Four times as much?
BASIL. Oh, easily!
FELIX. What are four times twenty-five pounds?
BASIL. One hundred.
FELIX. One hundred! (*Thoughtfully.*) Ach, so. I will not be long.
      (*He goes off* U.L. *through the archway.* NICOLETTE *to above table* D.L.)
NICOLETTE. Are you so sure that your friend will win the race?
BASIL. I'm a sportsman. I gamble!

NICOLETTE. I do not think he will win.
BASIL. I'm certain of it. He's in terrific form.
NICOLETTE. I hope you are speaking the truth—this time.
BASIL. What do you mean—this time?
NICOLETTE. Well, I was right about you not having a wife, wasn't I?
(*She goes out* L.)
    (*He watches her go, thoughtfully. He shrugs, moves away, looks back at door through which she went, shrugs again and moves up* C., *to look over the verandah.* PAULINE *comes on from the stairs* R. *She is wearing a delightful beach robe over her swimsuit, high-heeled sandals, a "coolie" hat and sun-glasses. She sits* L. *of table* D.R. BASIL *reacts to her appearance and watches her come down and sit at a table. He moves down and stands on her* L.C. *She does not take any notice of him.*)
BASIL (*brightly*). Good morning!
    (*She looks up at him, then looks away.*)
PAULINE (*coldly*). Good morning.
BASIL (*gazing at her in admiration*). Lovely!
PAULINE. I beg your pardon?
BASIL. The day—it's lovely!
PAULINE. I see.
BASIL. I say, I'm awfully sorry about—well, you know—last night.
PAULINE. That's all right. I'd forgotten about it.
BASIL (*eagerly*). You had?
PAULINE. Certainly.
BASIL. You mean you didn't mind my kissing you?
PAULINE. Of course I minded. But I'd forgotten about it. I always try to forget unpleasant things quickly.
BASIL. Was it *so* unpleasant? I don't know what came over me. It must be the spring.
PAULINE. What on earth have you done to your eye?
BASIL. Don't you remember?
PAULINE. You mean *I* did that?
BASIL. Yes.
PAULINE (*smiling for the first time*). I made a pretty good job of it, didn't I?
BASIL. Yes, you did!
PAULINE. Are you in the habit of going around kissing strange women like that?
BASIL. Well, not quite like that.
PAULINE. Oh?

BASIL. Sometimes they don't resist.
PAULINE (*surprised*). Really?
BASIL. No. As a matter of fact, sometimes they find me rather attractive. (*He beams at her. She looks him over coldly and turns away.*) Sometimes.
>(NICOLETTE *comes on from* L.C. *with two baskets of rolls, singing loudly, and comes to* C. BASIL *reacts crossly.*)

BASIL (*to her* R.). What do you want?
NICOLETTE. I have to lay the tables.
BASIL. Are you sure?
NICOLETTE. I have to lay the tables for breakfast. (*She puts a basket of rolls on the* C. *table.*)
BASIL. I thought you'd already done that?
NICOLETTE. I have not finished yet. (*She goes to table* D.L.)
BASIL. Couldn't you leave them—just for a while?
NICOLETTE. I have got my orders! I lay them now.
>(*She puts a basket of rolls on the table* D.L. *and goes off* L.C., *singing loudly. He watches her go, then moves quickly to* PAULINE.)

BASIL. I say, am I forgiven?
PAULINE (*disinterested*). H'm?
BASIL. Well—am I?
PAULINE. I suppose so.
BASIL. Oh, good! (*Moves nearer to her.*)
PAULINE. But that doesn't mean I'm encouraging you.
BASIL. Doesn't it?
PAULINE. No, it doesn't.
BASIL. Pity. Look, I—I wonder if—
>(NICOLETTE *comes on again with two more baskets of rolls, singing loudly. He moves away irritated to* U.C. *She goes above the table* C. *and below* BASIL *to table* U.R. *and puts a basket of rolls on it.*)

BASIL (*aside to* NICOLETTE). Will you go *away?*
NICOLETTE (*loudly*). Why should I go away?
>(*He tries to keep her quiet.*)

BASIL (*softly*). Will you please leave me alone for a moment?
NICOLETTE (*in a whisper*). Oh, very well. (*She crosses to above* PAULINE'S *table, puts down the other basket of rolls.*) He wishes to be left alone!
>(BASIL *is furious.* PAULINE *laughs.* NICOLETTE *goes off, singing.*)

BASIL (*laughs*). Sweet girl! (*Aside.*) I could kill her! (*To* L. *of* PAULINE.) Are you staying here very long?
PAULINE. I don't know for certain. A few days. Why?

BASIL. Oh, I just wondered. I'm staying for a few days, too.
PAULINE (*disinterested*). Really? How cosy.
BASIL. Quite a coincidence. Do you believe in—
PAULINE (*firmly*). No.
     (NICOLETTE *comes in again, singing.* BASIL *breaks to* C.)
NICOLETTE (*passing* BASIL). Excuse, please!
BASIL (*heavily*). Certainly!
NICOLETTE (*to* PAULINE). Are you going for a bathe before or after breakfast, Miss Maryot?
PAULINE. Before, I think, Nicolette.
BASIL (*to* L. *of* NICOLETTE). That's a good idea! I'll come, too.
NICOLETTE. What time did you say she would arrive, Mr. Basil?
BASIL. Who?
NICOLETTE. Your wife, of course!
     (BASIL *reacts.* PAULINE *smiles.*)
BASIL. What wife?
PAULINE. Have you got so many wives that you don't know what wife?
BASIL. I haven't got *any!*
NICOLETTE. The register says "Mr. and Mrs. Trent".
BASIL. I don't care what the register says. The register can mind its own business. I've never known a hotel register yet that spoke the truth!
NICOLETTE. Did you say she was blonde or brunette?
BASIL. I didn't say, and will you please go away!
NICOLETTE (*brightly*). Very well. I am going. (*She goes off* L.C.)
     (PAULINE *is enjoying the situation enormously.* BASIL *laughs awkwardly.*)
BASIL. She's always joking!
PAULINE (*rising and moving to* U.R.). I must go for my bathe.
BASIL (*up to* L. *of her*). I could be ready in a second.
PAULINE. But, Mr. Trent, you couldn't very well come and bathe with me. What would your wife say? (*She goes off* U.R.)
     (BASIL *to above wicker seat* C. NICOLETTE *returns from* L.C. *with three dishes of marmalade on a small tray.*)
BASIL. What did you have to go and do that for?
NICOLETTE (*innocently, as she puts marmalade on table* D.R.). Do what, Mister Basil?
BASIL (*to above* R. *end of wicker seat*). You know very well what I mean! Asking about my wife in front of her. You knew very well I'd got no wife.

NICOLETTE. Oh! I forgot! (*She crosses to table* C. *and puts down marmalade.*)
BASIL (*to* R. *of table* C.). You jolly well didn't. You did it deliberately. There I was, getting along splendidly—
NICOLETTE. You did not seem to be getting along splendidly when I saw you.
BASIL. There was plenty of time! Now, thanks to you, I'm as good as out of the game. Why did you do it?
NICOLETTE (*to table* D.L.). I do not think she is a good person for you. (*She puts down the last dish of marmalade.*)
BASIL. Why not?
NICOLETTE. I do not like the look of her.
   (*With a disapproving look, she goes off* L., *having finished laying the tables.* BASIL *goes up and looks in the direction* PAULINE *went.* HUMPHREY *comes unsteadily down the stairs. He is wearing grey trousers, the jacket of his blue suit and white tennis shoes. On his head is a straw boater.* BASIL *comes down to meet him* D.R.C.)
BASIL. Ah! So you decided to get up at last! And what a lovely morning, isn't it? Sun shining! Blue sky! Makes you glad to be alive!
HUMPHREY (*painfully*). Oh, do shut up! (*He crosses below* BASIL *to the chair* L. *of table* C., *each step obviously an agonizing effort.*)
BASIL. What's the matter with you?
HUMPHREY. What do you think's the matter with me? I'm stiff! I can hardly walk. That dreadful woman made me run so fast last night. I'm not used to that sort of thing.
BASIL. It'll pass off in time. You'll be a new man after a couple of days of that.
HUMPHREY. A couple of days! I knew I should never have left the L.B.F. and G.A.
BASIL. The what?
HUMPHREY. Little Bruddersford Fruiterers' and Greengrocers' Association.
BASIL (*joining in and assuming a North Country accent*). Fruiterers' and Greengrocers' Association! I say, you're not weakening, are you?
HUMPHREY. Yes, I am! I don't want to go through with all this deception. They're bound to find out sooner or later.
BASIL. Of course they are! But as long as it's later and not sooner, it's all right!
HUMPHREY. There'll be terrible trouble. (*Sits chair* L. *of table* C.)

BASIL (*to above* R. *end of table* C.). Well, you can't back out now. It's much too late. Besides, I've too much to lose.

HUMPHREY. You? What are *you* losing? I'm the one who stands to lose : my dignity, my self-respect—everything! It's all right for you. I'm the one who's left without the ladder!

BASIL. But you can't back out now. After all, your wife will be back, you know.

HUMPHREY. Oh, don't remind me!

BASIL. Just remember then—you try and back out now, and I'll tell your wife where you are. And who you're *with*.

HUMPHREY. But I'm not with anybody!

BASIL. No, I know—but *she'd* never believe that, would she? Not if I said I'd seen you and—the lady—together?

HUMPHREY. Oh—Christmas crackers!

BASIL. Now you'd better have your breakfast, because you can't stay here much longer. You shouldn't really have come down in the first place.

HUMPHREY. You surely don't expect me to remain upstairs in my room —cooped up like a chicken?

BASIL. Why not? That girl was here a moment ago.

HUMPHREY (*wearily*). Oh, what girl?

BASIL. The girl who's supposed to know you. She's gone for a bathe, but she'll be back in a minute. Suppose she sees you?

HUMPHREY. What about it?

BASIL. Well, she won't recognize you.

HUMPHREY. I don't care!

BASIL. But you're supposed to know her. She's come here to meet you—the real you.

HUMPHREY. I know!

BASIL (*sitting on the wicker seat*). So what happens when she comes face to face with you and doesn't recognize you? That'll give the game away.

HUMPHREY. And a good thing, too.

BASIL. Oh, no! You mustn't meet her, whatever happens. You'll have to hide whenever she appears.

(*At this moment* BRUCHIK *appears from* R., *dressed as before.* HUMPHREY *sees him, and watches with fascination as* BRUCHIK *comes down and stands* R. *of* BASIL, *who does not see him.* HUMPHREY *signals to* BASIL. *Business.*)

BASIL. I say, are you feeling all right?

HUMPHREY (*in a hushed whisper*). There's somebody standing just behind you.
BASIL. What? (*Turns, sees* BRUCHIK *and jumps.*) Oo! If we keep still he may go away.
   (*Pause.* BRUCHIK *remains expressionless.*)
He was more talkative last time.
HUMPHREY. Have you seen him before?
BASIL. Oh, yes. We had quite a conversation.
HUMPHREY. Perhaps you'd better speak, then.
BASIL. Yes, I suppose so. (*He turns to* BRUCHIK.) Good morning!
BRUCHIK. Good—morning!
   (*Pause.* BASIL *looks at* HUMPHREY.)
BASIL. Perhaps he'd like a drink. Here, this'll do.
   (BASIL *pours out a glass of orange juice and holds it out to* BRUCHIK, *who takes it and sniffs at it.*)
Orange juice.
BRUCHIK. Ah! Orange—juice! Good!
   (BASIL *nods to* HUMPHREY *in relief.* BRUCHIK *drinks the orange juice and extends glass to be replenished.*)
HUMPHREY (*tapping* BASIL'S *arm*). I think he wants some more.
BASIL. What? (*He turns to* BRUCHIK *and comes face to face with extended glass.*) Oh! Oh, yes. (*He refills the glass.*)
BRUCHIK. You!
BASIL. H'm?
BRUCHIK (*jabbing him with a finger*). You!
BASIL. Oh, all right. (*Pours a glass of orange juice for himself.*)
   (BRUCHIK *goes above the wicker seat to* R. *of* HUMPHREY.)
BRUCHIK. You, too!
HUMPHREY. Me?
BASIL. You heard him! (HUMPHREY *nervously goes and gets another glass from the table* D.L. *and then returns to his seat.* BASIL *pours him some orange juice.*)
BRUCHIK (*sitting* L. *of* BASIL *on wicker seat*). Now—ve drink!
   (*He turns to* BASIL *and they touch glasses with arms extended.*)
BRUCHIK. Prosit!
BASIL. Cheers.
   (BRUCHIK *suddenly links arms with* BASIL *in the Russian manner and drinks.* BASIL *cannot reach his glass as his arm is linked so firmly. Business.* BRUCHIK *then turns to* HUMPHREY.)
BRUCHIK. Cheers!

HUMPHREY. Oh—er—yes.

(BRUCHIK *repeats the previous business with* HUMPHREY, *who is pulled so roughly towards* BRUCHIK *that his chair goes up on to two legs.*)

BRUCHIK (*smiling delightedly*). Good!

(*There is a long pause as* BRUCHIK *studies each of them in turn. They squirm apprehensively under his scrutiny, and* HUMPHREY *hums nervously.*)

(*Conclusively.*) You are English!

BASIL. I say, well done!

BRUCHIK. You are perhaps here for the Olympic Games?

BASIL. Oh, yes, rather!

BRUCHIK (*to* BASIL). You are the English runner who is staying here?

BASIL. Me? No, not me—him.

BRUCHIK (*turning to regard* HUMPHREY *without enthusiasm*). Him?

BASIL. Yes.

(BRUCHIK *laughs loudly.* HUMPHREY *squirms.*)

BRUCHIK (*pointing*). Him?

BASIL. Yes.

(BRUCHIK *laughs even louder.*)

BRUCHIK (*through his laughter*). Him?

BASIL. Yes! (*Caught up by* BRUCHIK'S *laughter, he begins to laugh also.*)

BRUCHIK. The man who is expected to win the five thousand metres?

BASIL. Yes!

(*They both roar with laughter, arms round each other's shoulders.* HUMPHREY *sits still, rather pathetically.* BRUCHIK *suddenly stops laughing and puts his face closer to* BASIL'S. BASIL'S *laughter checks abruptly.*)

BRUCHIK. You are telling me lies!

BASIL. No, I'm not.

BRUCHIK. Good. (*Looks at* HUMPHREY, *smiles, raises his orange juice.*) Ve vill vin!

(*He roars again and slaps* HUMPHREY *on the back.* HUMPHREY *falls on to the ground.* BASIL *goes round and helps him up and dusts him down.* BRUCHIK *goes round* R. *end of table* C. *to* D.C.)

BRUCHIK. You are looking forward to the Games?

HUMPHREY. No! Not a bit!

BRUCHIK. No?

BASIL. Yes, of course he is!

BRUCHIK. You will enjoy the Games?

HUMPHREY. No.
BASIL. Yes, of course he will!
BRUCHIK. You don't look as if you were going to enjoy them.
BASIL. No, he doesn't, does he? You heard what he said—look as if you were going to enjoy the Games.
(HUMPHREY *forces a broad smile*.)
There! That's better! See?
BRUCHIK. Yes. I see.
BASIL (*crossing to* L. *of* BRUCHIK). We English take our games very seriously, you know. (*Looks back at* HUMPHREY.) All right, you can stop now.
(HUMPHREY *relaxes*.)
BRUCHIK. You are his manager?
BASIL. Er—well—yes, I am.
BRUCHIK. Then tell me—what is his best for the mile?
BASIL. The mile.
BRUCHIK. Yes.
BASIL. H'm, now let me see—the mile. (*To* HUMPHREY.) You've run a mile, haven't you? Er—oh, it's pretty good.
BRUCHIK. How good?
BASIL. Oh—above average.
BRUCHIK. What time?
BASIL. H'm?
BRUCHIK. What time?
BASIL (*looks at watch*). A quarter past nine.
BRUCHIK (*loudly*). What time for ze mile!
BASIL. Oh, for ze mile? (*To* R. *of* HUMPHREY.) What would *you* say?
HUMPHREY (*triumphantly*). How can I run and look at a watch at the same time?
BASIL (*pushing* HUMPHREY). Yes, you would say that!
BRUCHIK (*suspiciously*). I don't think he has run a mile at all.
BASIL (*returning to* L. *of* BRUCHIK). Of course he has! He's done it lots of times.
BRUCHIK. Then how long does he take to run it?
BASIL (*plunging in*). Three minutes.
BRUCHIK. *Three* minutes?
BASIL. Yes.
BRUCHIK. Flat?
BASIL. Well, it takes him longer over hurdles.
BRUCHIK. I mean three minutes *exactly*?

BASIL. Oh, give a second, take a second!
BRUCHIK. The world record is just under *four* minutes.
BASIL. Not any more. He's been practising!
BRUCHIK. I think you are making fun of me.
BASIL. No fear!
BRUCHIK. Well, you had better not.
   (BRUCHIK *crosses to* HUMPHREY *and circles round him, looking him over.* HUMPHREY *retreats towards the chair* L. *of table* C.)
BRUCHIK. Now I go and practice—Mister Three-Minute Mile!
   (*He laughs loudly and runs off* U.R., BASIL *quickly dodging out of his path.* HUMPHREY *subsides into his chair.*)
BASIL (*sitting* L. *end of wicker seat*). That's the man you've got to beat!
HUMPHREY (*painfully*). I know! (*Rises.*) It's no good. I can't go through with it. I'm going to pack my things and go home.
BASIL (*stretching out on the wicker seat*). All right.
HUMPHREY (*surprised*). What?
BASIL. Back you go to the Little Bruddersford Fruiterers' and Greengrocers' Association. I thought it was all talk last night.
HUMPHREY. What was?
BASIL. All that stuff about rebelling against order and routine—kicking over the traces—all that. Here's your chance to make people respect you. Even her.
HUMPHREY. Who?
BASIL. Your wife. You go back now she'll have you exactly where she wants you. Your life won't be worth living.
HUMPHREY. When you put it like that, of course, I feel I really *ought* to stay. You mean people really *will* look up to me and respect me?
BASIL (*sitting up*). You'll be the toast of the town!
HUMPHREY. That's all very well, but you forget—I can't run.
BASIL. You can run enough.
HUMPHREY. Not enough to win.
BASIL (*rising and moving to* R.C.). Who said anything about winning?
HUMPHREY. You mean—?
BASIL. Be the glorious loser! If you're a sportsman that's just as good as winning. All you have to do is to take your time—and lose.
HUMPHREY (*suspiciously, to below table* C.). You *want* me to lose!
BASIL. No, no, but—
HUMPHREY. You do! You *want* me to lose this race!
BASIL. I'm only being realistic.
HUMPHREY. You want me to lose this race deliberately!

BASIL. Of course I don't! You do your best. I don't mind. You'll still lose.

(FELIX *comes in from* U.L.)

FELIX. Everything is arranged, m'sieur! I saw the gentleman.
BASIL (*quickly*). Yes, all right, thank you, Felix!
HUMPHREY (*to* L. *of* BASIL). What is arranged?
BASIL. Oh, nothing important.
FELIX (*to* C.). I can understand m'sieur not wishing his wife to be here. She is very beautiful.
HUMPHREY. My wife?
FELIX. No, no! Your—friend.
HUMPHREY. What friend?
FELIX. Why, Miss Maryot, of course, who arrived last night to see you. She is very beautiful. You are a very lucky man.
BASIL. He doesn't know how lucky!
FELIX. You are a bit of a dark horse, m'sieur. I saw her just now. She is returning from her bathe.
BASIL. Oh, is she? That'll never do, will it?
FELIX. Why not?
BASIL. Well—he wants to change.
FELIX (*smiling delightedly*). Oh, yes! Of course!
HUMPHREY. I *don't* want to change!
BASIL. Don't be silly—of course you do. You look terrible. Just look at those trousers! You wouldn't want to meet a lady looking like that, would you?
HUMPHREY. I don't care!
BASIL. Of course you do. Go and slip into something dashing. (*Forcing* HUMPHREY *off* R.)
HUMPHREY. I don't feel dashing! (*Exit* HUMPHREY *upstairs*.)
FELIX. He is such a reluctant lover!
BASIL. Yes. Isn't he? Look, will you go and keep an eye out for Mrs. Podmore? We don't want her turning up now.
FELIX. Yes, of course. But I already have one eye out for that lady. I do not want another!

(BASIL *goes quickly off* R. *after* HUMPHREY. FELIX *starts to go* L. *as* PAULINE *comes on from* U.L., *dressed as before, having come from her bathe. She comes to below the table* C.)

Did you have a good bathe?
PAULINE. Yes, thank you.
FELIX. Perhaps you would like your coffee now?

PAULINE. Yes, please.
FELIX. Ah, good. I will tell Nicolette. (*Pause.*) He will be down in a moment.
PAULINE. H'm?
FELIX. Your friend—the English runner.
PAULINE. Oh, good. I haven't had the chance to see him at all yet. He must have been still in bed when I went for my bathe.
FELIX. I expect you are looking forward to seeing him?
PAULINE. Yes, indeed. It will be nice to talk over old times.

(HUMPHREY *enters cautiously from* R. *looking off the way he has come. He is obviously avoiding* BASIL. *He does not see* PAULINE *or* FELIX.)

FELIX (*aside to* PAULINE). Ah! here he is! I will leave you. I must keep out the eye for the wife! (*Exit.*)

(HUMPHREY *gets to* L. *of the table* D.R. *before he turns and sees* PAULINE. *He is panic-stricken but it is too late to hide. He waits for expected explosion. To his surprise,* PAULINE *smiles broadly and advances on him with outstretched arms.*)

PAULINE. Darling!

(*He glances behind himself to see if there is anyone else there to whom she can be talking.* PAULINE *embraces him. He is bewildered and alarmed. They meet* L. *of table* D.R.)

It's wonderful to see you!
HUMPHREY. Oh, dear.
PAULINE. You haven't changed a bit.
HUMPHREY. Are you quite sure?
PAULINE. Let me have a look at you.

(*He pivots in spite of himself. She gazes at him in admiration.*)

M'm. I knew you wouldn't be any different from last year.
HUMPHREY. What was I like last year?
PAULINE. I don't have to tell *you!* (*Linking his arm.*)
HUMPHREY. No, of course not. But I wish you would.
PAULINE. Come and sit down.
HUMPHREY. Well, actually, I have to—
PAULINE. Nonsense! Come on.

(*He sits reluctantly next to her on the wicker seat, she* L. *end, he* R. *end. She sits very close to him. Business. He puts his straw boater over her knees for a moment.*)

When did you get here?

HUMPHREY. Last night.
PAULINE. You mean you were here when I arrived?
HUMPHREY. Well—yes, I was.
PAULINE. And you didn't come out to meet me!
HUMPHREY. I might not have recognized you.
PAULINE. Could you forget me so soon?
HUMPHREY. Oh, no! Of course not. It was your hat. You looked different with your hat on.
PAULINE. Then you *did* see me arrive!
HUMPHREY. Well, yes, I did have a peek.
PAULINE. And you didn't speak?
HUMPHREY. It was only a brief peek.

(NICOLETTE *comes on from* L.C. *with a jug of coffee and a jug of hot milk. She reacts to the scene.*)

NICOLETTE. Your coffee, miss.
PAULINE. Oh, thank you, Nicolette. I'll have it here.

(NICOLETTE *puts down the coffee. She goes, with a backward surprised glance.*

PAULINE *makes sure that* NICOLETTE *is out of ear-shot, and then speaks confidentially.*)

PAULINE. It's all clear.
HUMPHREY (*puzzled*). Oh? Oh, good!
PAULINE. It was a good idea choosing this place.
HUMPHREY. Yes. It was rather, wasn't it?
PAULINE. Was it *your* idea?
HUMPHREY. Well, in a way, I suppose it was, really.
PAULINE. Brilliant!
HUMPHREY (*pleased*). Do you really think so?
PAULINE. And daring!
HUMPHREY. Well, I wouldn't go so far as to say that.
PAULINE. You must be very brave!
HUMPHREY (*modestly*). Oh, it's nothing, really.

(*He leans back against her without thinking, and* PAULINE *puts an arm around his shoulders.* BASIL *enters in a hurry from* R. *He stops and takes in the scene.*)

BASIL. Oh, I beg your pardon! (*And he goes out again, bewildered.*)
PAULINE. Do you know that man?
HUMPHREY. We met yesterday.
PAULINE. You're sure he doesn't suspect anything?
HUMPHREY. Suspect anything?

PAULINE. No, of course not. You're far too clever for that. You arranged everything beautifully.
HUMPHREY. Oh, thank you.
PAULINE (*rising*). Now I must go.
HUMPHREY (*rising*). Oh, good!
PAULINE. What?
HUMPHREY. I said "Oh, good"—I mean the sooner you go—the sooner you'll be back!
PAULINE. How sweet!
    (*She kisses the top of his head impulsively.*)
 I shall see you later. (*She crosses him to* R.C.) Everything is all right for tonight, isn't it?
HUMPHREY. H'm?
PAULINE. You did *say* tonight, didn't you?
HUMPHREY. Oh?
    (*She moves to the stairs and turns.*)
PAULINE. Till tonight!
    (*She waves to him and goes off* R. HUMPHREY *is nonplussed. He sits very still and gazes blankly in front of him.* BASIL *returns to* R. *of* HUMPHREY.)
BASIL. Well! You seemed to be getting on like a house on fire! I thought you were supposed to hide whenever she appeared? I say, you're not dead, are you? (*Feels the top of his head.*) Oh, no. Still warm. Look, why didn't you hide?
HUMPHREY. There wasn't time.
BASIL. Well, anyhow, there was no need to talk to her.
HUMPHREY. She recognized me.
BASIL. You should have left as soon as— What did you say?
HUMPHREY. I said she recognized me.
BASIL. Stop acting the giddy goat!
HUMPHREY. I'm *not* acting the giddy goat!
BASIL. She *couldn't* have recognized you.
HUMPHREY. She *did*.
BASIL. But she doesn't know you.
HUMPHREY. She thinks she does.
BASIL. But she saw the real you a year ago.
HUMPHREY. I know.
BASIL. So how can she possibly mistake you for him?
HUMPHREY. I don't know.
BASIL. Are you quite sure you're telling me the truth?

HUMPHREY. Of course I'm sure! She came up to me as if she'd known me for years. You saw us talking together. I didn't know what to do.

BASIL. You seemed to be doing all right. I say, you haven't been hiding anything from me, have you?

HUMPHREY. What do you mean?

BASIL. You're quite *sure* you don't know this girl?

HUMPHREY. Of course I don't know her.

BASIL. I mean, I wouldn't blame you if you did. She looks all right.

HUMPHREY. What are you suggesting?

BASIL. Well, it wouldn't be impossible, would it? You come out to the Continent, leaving your wife behind. You might easily have something else lined up over here.

HUMPHREY. Do I look the sort of man who—who— Oh, it's unthinkable!

BASIL. Oh, I dunno. You might be a wolf in sheep's wotnot for all I know.

HUMPHREY. I tell you I don't know this girl. I've never seen her before in my life.

BASIL. Then why does she pretend to know you? You must admit it all sounds a little fishy. I wouldn't be at all surprised if you were a dirty old man!

(FELIX *comes rushing in from* U.L.)

FELIX. She is here!

BASIL. Quickly! You'd better hide!

HUMPHREY. Where?

BASIL. Oh, anywhere! Under the table!

(*He pushes the protesting* HUMPHREY *under the table* D.R., *and pulls the table cloth to hide him.* BASIL *then returns to* C. AGNES *strides on from* U.L. *She carries a suitcase which she puts down defiantly* L. *of table* C.)

AGNES. I'm here to stay!

BASIL. How delightful!

FELIX. But we have no room.

BASIL. Ah! We have no room.

AGNES. Then you'll have to find me one.

FELIX. Impossible, madame!

AGNES. Nothing's impossible if you put your mind to it. (*To* BASIL.) What about *your* room?

BASIL. I think we'd be a little cramped in there.

AGNES. You know what I mean. I know Humphrey's here, and I intend to remain here until I find him.

FELIX. You must be mistaken, madame.

AGNES. I am not mistaken! I saw him last night. What he thought he was doing in those ridiculous shorts I don't know, but I do know he's here. And he's got a lot to answer for!

(*She pounds down* R. *as far as the table under which* HUMPHREY *is hiding.*)

And when I find him, he'll be sorry!

(*As she faces* L., *the table behind her begins to move slowly farther* R.)

What number is his room?

FELIX (*in to below table* C.). I assure, you, madame, he is not in his room.

AGNES. What?

FELIX. I mean, he has not *got* a room in this hotel.

(*The table moves again.*)

AGNES (*to between them at* C.). Let me have a look at that register.

BASIL. Oh, I'm sorry, we don't allow that.

AGNES. What's it got to do with you?

BASIL. That register is strictly private.

(NICOLETTE *comes in from* L.)

AGNES (*below* FELIX *to* D.L. *of him*). Hey! you!

NICOLETTE. Yes, madame!

AGNES. What room is my husband in?

NICOLETTE. Your husband?

AGNES. Humphrey Podmore. Or he may be calling himself Smith.

NICOLETTE. Ah! Smith!

(BASIL *and* FELIX *signal frantically to her.* AGNES *turns and sees them, and they pretend to be playing "pat-a-cake".*)

NICOLETTE. What does he look like?

AGNES. Short, bald and respectable.

NICOLETTE. Yes, we have someone here who is bald.

(BASIL *and* FELIX *are panic-stricken.*)

But I do not think he is respectable.

AGNES. He may have changed. What is the number of his room?

NICOLETTE (*having caught on to the frantic signals*). But this man is also very tall.

(BASIL *and* FELIX *relax.*)

AGNES. Are you sure?

NICOLETTE. Oh, yes. He could not be your husband.

(NICOLETTE *suddenly notices the table* D.R. *is out of position.*)
Who has moved that table?
   (*Before they can stop her she has moved straight across to the table. She straightens the tablecloth and moves the table, revealing* HUMPHREY. *She utters a little cry. At the same time,* BASIL *and* FELIX *come down on either side of* AGNES, *each take an arm, and walk her swiftly* D.L. *so that her back is to* HUMPHREY. HUMPHREY *signals to* NICOLETTE *to keep quiet and rushes off* R. AGNES, *hearing a noise, turns quickly but is just too late to see* HUMPHREY. BASIL *and* FELIX *shake hands.* NICOLETTE *is transfixed.*)

AGNES. Who was that?
BASIL. A school friend of mine.
AGNES. You seem to have a lot of school friends here.
BASIL. Yes. It's an Old Boys Reunion.
   (NICOLETTE *replaces the table* D.R. *and tidies it. Then she gets to* D.R. *of table* C.)
AGNES (*sitting above table* C.). I shall remain here until you find me a room.
   (BASIL *and* FELIX *exchange looks*)
BASIL (*moving to* L. *of her*). Even if we had a room, madame, there are other things to consider.
AGNES. What do you mean?
BASIL. Customs.
AGNES. What customs?
BASIL. *The* Customs. Before staying in this hotel, all baggage must be examined.
AGNES. What for?
BASIL (*confidentially*). Contraband!
AGNES. Don't be ridiculous!
BASIL. You see, just lately, there's been rather a lot of smuggling. All sorts of things have been smuggled. (*Looking at* FELIX.) Jewellery, brandy.
FELIX (*catching on*). Oh, yes, m'sieur—brandy! A great deal of brandy!
   (FELIX *beckons to* NICOLETTE *and whispers to her. She goes off* D.L.)
BASIL. So you see, all bags must be examined.
AGNES. Who says so?
BASIL (*to* FELIX). Who says so? Oh, it's—it's written here. (*He takes down the motto from the wall.*)
AGNES. Let me see that!

(*He quickly waves it under her nose.*)

BASIL. It's not in English. I'll translate it for you. (*Pretending to read.*) "All baggage must be examined for contraband before any reservations may be accepted." There we are!

AGNES. Who is it signed by?

BASIL (*looking closely at the motto*). H. M. Humperdink.

AGNES. Who's he?

BASIL. He's a big man in the police department. Isn't he, Felix?

FELIX. A very big man, m'sieur.

(BASIL *hands the motto to* FELIX.)

BASIL. So now I must examine your bag.

AGNES. What's it got to do with you, anyway?

BASIL. I'm the customs officer. Your bag, please.

AGNES. I refuse!

(*He takes it quickly and stands above the chair* L. *of table to* C. *to open it.*)

(*Rising.*) Leave that alone! How dare you!

BASIL. Now, now! Naughty, naughty! Ah! what have we here? (*He produces a large undergarment.*)

AGNES. Put that back! At once!

BASIL. All right! Don't get excited.

(NICOLETTE *returns with a bottle of brandy behind her back.*)

Now, Nicolette, would you take madame over there and search her, please?

AGNES. Search me! I'll call the police!

BASIL. It has to be done.

AGNES. Nonsense! That isn't what it said on the notice.

BASIL. Isn't it? Let's have a look. (*Looks at motto.*) Yes, it does—quite clearly—*all* bags must be examined.

AGNES (*moving away* R. *slightly*). I refuse to be searched! I'll call the police.

(*As she faces the other way,* NICOLETTE *passes the brandy to* FELIX, *who in turn passes it to* BASIL *who puts it in the case.*)

BASIL (*ominously*). Yes. I think you'd better.

AGNES. What do you mean by that?

BASIL. Madame, I am surprised. Surprised and shocked.

AGNES. What are you talking about?

(*He produces a bottle of brandy from her suitcase. She stares at it.*)

AGNES. How did that get in there?

BASIL. How indeed!
AGNES. You put it there! You put it there deliberately!
BASIL. Really, what an accusation. I shall have to report this, of course.
AGNES. All right—go on—report me!
BASIL (*taken aback*). What?
AGNES. Go ahead! I don't mind!
BASIL. You could go to prison.
AGNES. I could, but I don't think I shall. (*She collects her suitcase after closing the lid, etc.*) Now, having suffered this indignity—show me to my room!
FELIX. But there is no room!
AGNES. Then why did you search my bag? Show me to my room. Or shall I call the police.
FELIX. Yes, madame. This way, madame.
    (FELIX *gestures to* L. AGNES *follows him to* L. *and turns.* NICOLETTE *is below the* L.C. *exit.*)
AGNES. You haven't heard the last of this, you know. My property, I think!
    (*She grabs the bottle of brandy from* BASIL *and goes off* L.C. *followed by* FELIX. BASIL *moves down to* NICOLETTE *above the table* D.L.)
BASIL. Oh—er—thanks for helping us out.
NICOLETTE. That is all right.
    (*Pause. He moves nearer to her.*)
BASIL. Why did you?
    (*She looks up at him, then down again.*)
NICOLETTE. I do not know.
BASIL. I thought at first you were going to give the game away.
NICOLETTE. My father seemed to want me to help—so I help.
BASIL. *Only* because of your father?
NICOLETTE (*gently*). I did not do it for you.
BASIL (*with a smile*). Oh, I know! I didn't think that you would.
NICOLETTE (*firmly*). I did *not*.
BASIL. All right. But thank you anyway.
    (PAULINE *comes down the stairs, having changed into a summer dress.*)
PAULINE. Well, I certainly feel ready for my breakfast now, Nicolette.
NICOLETTE. I will get you some more coffee. (*Exit* L.)
    (PAULINE *sits* R. *of table* D.R. *and eats rolls and marmalade, etc.*

BASIL *comes and stands near to her. He coughs noticeably, but she does not react. Pause.*)

BASIL. Nothing like the good old summer—*I* always say. What do *you* always say?

PAULINE. Go away!

BASIL. That's what I thought!

(*He starts to run off up the steps* R., *as* FELIX *runs on from* U.L., *talking.*)

FELIX. All is well! I locked the old lady in her room and—

BASIL. S'sh!

(FELIX *stops abruptly, and they both run off,* L. *and* R. *respectively.* PAULINE *shrugs, continues eating. After a moment,* BRUCHIK *returns from* U.L., *glances off* L., *and then moves down to* L. *of her table. She still takes no notice.* BRUCHIK *sits at her table. After a moment, she speaks, without looking up. They are both extremely furtive and sinister in this scene.*)

PAULINE. He's here.

BRUCHIK. Good. When?

PAULINE. He arrived last night.

BRUCHIK. Good.

(NICOLETTE *comes on with coffee. She sets it down, reacts to* BRUCHIK's *presence.*)

NICOLETTE. You wish your coffee now?

BRUCHIK. If you please.

NICOLETTE (*pointedly*). At *this* table?

BRUCHIK. If madame does not object.

PAULINE. Of course I don't object.

(*Exit* NICOLETTE L.C. *Simultaneously,* BRUCHIK *pours coffee into* PAULINE's *cup as she pours milk into his.*)

BRUCHIK (*cautiously*). Which one is our man?

PAULINE. The English runner?

BRUCHIK. With the bald head?

PAULINE. Yes.

BRUCHIK. I thought there was something strange about him.

PAULINE. He's an impostor.

BRUCHIK. What happened to the *real* runner?

PAULINE. He was—removed. Our people provided this replacement.

BRUCHIK. Good. Very good. Have you spoken to him?

PAULINE. Yes. We kept to general conversation at the first meeting to avoid arousing suspicion. I must say he excelled at general conversation! When I mentioned tonight, he seemed genuinely surprised.

BRUCHIK. Good. They have obviously sent one of their best men. What about the man with him?

PAULINE. Apparently they only met here. I don't think there is any worry about him.

BRUCHIK. Good.

(NICOLETTE *brings in the coffee, sets it down and goes out again. They wait until she is out of ear-shot. Simultaneously, she pours coffee into his cup as he pours milk into hers.*)

BRUCHIK. What is the next move?

PAULINE. The next move is up to you. You must establish contact and he will tell you exactly where and when he intends to hand over the stuff.

BRUCHIK. I see. How will he recognize me?

PAULINE. When you meet him you say "The robin is on the bough".

BRUCHIK. The robin?

PAULINE. Is on the bough.

BRUCHIK. Good. I will remember. "The robin is on the bough."

(HUMPHREY *appears from the stairs, looking about cautiously. He carries a newspaper.*)

PAULINE. Here he comes! I'll leave you with him.

(*She rises and crosses to* R. HUMPHREY *turns and sees her there. He jumps with surprise.*)

HUMPHREY. Oh! Hullo!

PAULINE. Hullo.

(*She pinches his cheek and goes off* R. HUMPHREY *descends the steps and crosses to* R.C., *then he sees* BRUCHIK.)

HUMPHREY. Oh, good morning!

BRUCHIK. Good morning.

(HUMPHREY *starts to go.*)

Do not go!

(HUMPHREY *stops.*)

BRUCHIK. Come and sit down.

HUMPHREY (*nervously*). Oh, very well.

(HUMPHREY *thinks of sitting at the table* D.R., *changes his mind and goes and sits* L. *of table* C. *He puts the newspaper up in front of his face to read.*)

BRUCHIK. Where is your friend?

HUMPHREY. I don't know.

(BRUCHIK *looks around cautiously and comes nearer to* HUMPHREY *to* R. *of table* C.)

BRUCHIK. The robin is on the bough.

(HUMPHREY *lowers the newspaper slowly.*)

HUMPHREY. I beg your pardon.

BRUCHIK. The robin is on the bough.

HUMPHREY (*after glancing over his* L. *shoulder*). Which bough?

BRUCHIK (*puzzled*). I do not know.

HUMPHREY (*knowingly*). Ah! well, there you are then! (*He puts the newspaper up again.*)

(*Pause.* BRUCHIK *decides to try again. He sits* R. *end of wicker seat.*)

BRUCHIK. The robin is on the bough.

(HUMPHREY *lowers the paper slowly.*)

HUMPHREY. Yes, I know. You just told me.

BRUCHIK. Well, that is all right, then?

HUMPHREY. It is as far as I'm concerned. Why shouldn't it be all right?

BRUCHIK. Then we can talk?

HUMPHREY. If you want to. (*He puts down the paper.*) What shall we talk *about*?

BRUCHIK. Does anyone suspect?

HUMPHREY. Suspect what?

BRUCHIK. That you are an impostor.

HUMPHREY (*guiltily*). S'sh! You mean you know?

BRUCHIK. Of course!

HUMPHREY. How did you guess?

BRUCHIK. It was easy.

HUMPHREY. You won't tell anyone?

BRUCHIK. That would not be very wise.

HUMPHREY. You see, they expect me to win. Oh, I can't go through with it! I've got to get away from here.

BRUCHIK. That could be arranged.

HUMPHREY. You mean you'll really help me?

BRUCHIK. But of course! That is what I am here for. (*He is puzzled by* HUMPHREY'S *reactions.*)

HUMPHREY. Well, I must say I think that's very kind of you. (*He gives a little laugh, rises and sits next to* BRUCHIK.) I never imagined you were

like this! You're really rather a decent sort of chap! Now, what do do you suggest?
BRUCHIK. Everything is in your room?
HUMPHREY. Oh, yes! I didn't unpack very much. I can be ready in a few minutes. (*He hesitates.*)
BRUCHIK. What is the matter?
HUMPHREY. Well, you see—the young man who said he was my manager—he insists that I run in the Games here. He's a very determined young man. He mustn't find out that I'm leaving, or he'll make it very unpleasant for me.
BRUCHIK. Do not worry. We will keep him out of the way.
HUMPHREY. Oh, thank you so much! I must say you're being awfully helpful, and I do appreciate it. It really is jolly kind of you.
BRUCHIK (*rising abruptly*). Now I must arrange everything. Tomorrow morning you will get away from here.
HUMPHREY. Oh, thank you.
BRUCHIK (*turning at foot of stairs*). Let me have the stuff tonight. (*He goes off upstairs.*)

(HUMPHREY *watches him go, bewildered.*)

HUMPHREY. The stuff? What an extraordinary fellow! (*He giggles thoughtfully and puts up his newspaper again.*)

(*After a moment* PAULINE *returns. She comes up to his* R. *and starts to read something on the back of the newspaper. He lowers the paper slowly, sees her and utters a nervous giggle.*)

Oh, there you are!
PAULINE. May I sit down?
HUMPHREY. Somebody might come in and see us.
PAULINE. You know, I think you're rather sweet.
HUMPHREY. Oh, do you?

(*She sits close to him.*)

PAULINE. *Very* sweet.
HUMPHREY. Oh, thank you.
PAULINE. And very clever.
HUMPHREY. Oh, I don't know.
PAULINE (*playing with the back of his head*). And very attractive.
HUMPHREY. Oh, fiddle-faddle!

(*At this moment* AGNES *pounds on from* L. *She is a trifle dishevelled.*)

AGNES. Humphrey!

(HUMPHREY *and* PAULINE *spring apart and rise.* PAULINE *to* L. *of table* D.R., HUMPHREY *to above table* C.)

So I've found you at last!

(*He edges to* R. *of table* C.)

HUMPHREY. Oh, hullo, dear.

AGNES. I suppose you thought you'd got away from me?

HUMPHREY. Yes, dear. I mean, no, dear.

AGNES. I'm not such a fool as I look.

HUMPHREY. No, dear—I mean, yes, dear—I mean, oh dear!

AGNES. Who's this?

HUMPHREY. What, dear?

AGNES. Are you deaf all of a sudden?

HUMPHREY. No, dear.

AGNES. Then why do you keep pretending you haven't heard?

HUMPHREY. It gives me time to think.

AGNES (*below* HUMPHREY *to* L. *of* PAULINE). So you're the reason he left home, eh?

HUMPHREY (*to* L. *of* AGNES). This is Miss—er—Pauline.

AGNES. So he ran away with you, eh?

PAULINE. I only met him this morning.

AGNES. Oh, you did, eh? He arrives last night, and you pick him up this morning! Well, I'll tell you this much—I don't think much of your choice.

HUMPHREY. Oh, look, my dear.

AGNES (*swinging on him*). Yours isn't much better!

(FELIX *runs on from* L.C.)

FELIX (*entering*). She has got away! (*Sees* AGNES.) Ah! bonjour! bonjour! bonjour!

AGNES (*to* R. *of* FELIX). And I've got a bone to pick with *you*, too!

FELIX. But, madame, it was not my fault.

AGNES. Not your fault? I suppose it was only by accident that you locked me in my room?

PAULINE (*aside to* HUMPHREY). We will arrange everything. Tonight!

(*She plants a kiss on his brow, just as* AGNES *turns and sees her.*)

AGNES. Cut that out! We don't want any of that here!

(*Exit* PAULINE *upstairs.* AGNES *advances on* HUMPHREY *and peers at him closely. He squirms.*)

I don't know what's got into you. I don't really. Have you been taking something? (*She turns to* FELIX.) And as for you, I'm going to sue you for assault and battery.

FELIX. But it was a mistake! I did not mean to lock the door!

AGNES (*holding the lower part of her back*). It was a very hazardous job getting out of that window.

(BASIL *comes on from stairs to* D.R.)

BASIL. Well, I say, what a happy little gathering! (*Sees* AGNES.) Oh, my God!

AGNES. You seem surprised to see me.

BASIL (*to* R. *of* HUMPHREY). Not at all. I had a feeling you'd get out somehow.

(FELIX *"shushes" him, and* AGNES *turns and glares at* FELIX. *She then goes to* HUMPHREY.)

AGNES. Are you packed, Podmore?

HUMPHREY. I never *un*packed.

BASIL. There! Isn't that pathetic? (*He breathes on* HUMPHREY'S *head and polishes it with his sleeve.*)

AGNES. We're leaving.

BASIL. Oh, you can't do that!

AGNES. Why not?

BASIL. You've only just arrived.

AGNES. And now we're leaving. Come on, Humphrey! There's a train in half an hour. We shall be on it. Go and get your bag.

(HUMPHREY *is silent.*)

Did you hear me?

BASIL. Humphrey, did you hear her?

HUMPHREY. Yes. I heard her.

AGNES. Humphrey! Come along! Where's your room?

BASIL. It's now or never, Humphrey.

AGNES. Humphrey, for the last time, come along!

HUMPHREY (*meekly*). Yes, dear.

BASIL (*astounded*). Yes, dear?

AGNES. That's better. Which is your room?

BASIL (*threateningly*). Humphrey, isn't your room the one with all that luggage in? Perhaps I ought to get the police to come and help you move your luggage, eh?

(HUMPHREY *looks at him in horror. After a moment he makes up his mind.*)

HUMPHREY. This way, my dear.

(*He leads her across to the door to the wine cellar* D.L. BASIL *and* FELIX *realize that he is sending her the wrong way.* FELIX *opens the door to the wine cellar.*)

FELIX. This way, madame.

AGNES (*peering into the room*). Looks pretty dark. This isn't another of your tricks, is it?

(HUMPHREY *suddenly gives her a push into the room, and* FELIX *closes and bolts the door.*)

HUMPHREY (*to* C.). Oh, dear! What *have* I done?

(BASIL *shakes him by the hand.*)

FELIX. I will go and make sure that there is *no* way she can get out this time!

(*He goes off* L.C., *chuckling delightedly. From within* AGNES *pounds on the door.*)

AGNES (*off*). Let me out! Let me out!

HUMPHREY (*to* L. *of table* D.R.). She'll never forgive me for this—never! Never as long as I live!

BASIL. You ought to get a gold medal for this. It's the only one you *will* get.

(*From* U.L. *comes a little man carrying a small suitcase. The* VISITOR *is rather dishevelled and has a piece of plaster on his forehead. He comes down to* L. *of* BASIL.)

Don't you worry. She'll get over it in time. (*Turns and sees the* VISITOR. *To* HUMPHREY.) What's that? Good morning. Who are you?

VISITOR. I hope I've come to the right place.

BASIL. We're full up.

VISITOR. But I have a reservation. I'm sorry I'm so late, but I had a slight accident and missed my train.

BASIL. What sort of accident?

VISITOR. I was knocked over the head.

BASIL. Really? Oh, yes! I see! Well, what are you doing here?

VISITOR. I'm running in the Olympic Games. My name is Joe Smith.

BASIL. Oh, no, it's not.

VISITOR. I beg your pardon?

BASIL. You can't possibly be Joe Smith.

VISITOR. Why not?

BASIL. Because this is Joe Smith! (*Points to* HUMPHREY.)

(*Enter* FELIX.)

Ah! Felix!

FELIX. Monsieur?

BASIL. Room for one more inside? (*Signals to* FELIX.)

FELIX. H'm? Oh! Oh, yes—of course, m'sieur!

HUMPHREY. Oh, no!

(FELIX *opens the door to the wine cellar and* BASIL *pushes the* VISITOR *protesting inside.* FELIX *locks the door. From within we hear protestations from* AGNES.)

HUMPHREY. But my wife's in there!

BASIL. That's all right. They can keep each other company!

HUMPHREY. Oooh! (*Sits despondently* L. *of table* D.R. *and sinks his head into his hands.*)

QUICK CURTAIN

ACT THREE

The following afternoon. The tables are no longer laid.

MISS HACKET *is on her back* C., *doing "bicycling" exercises.*
NICOLETTE *enters from* L.C., *sees* MISS HACKET *and comes round to*
R. *of her.*

MISS HACKET (*sitting up*). Have you seen him anywhere?
NICOLETTE. Mister Smiss?
MISS HACKET. Yes.
NICOLETTE. No. I have not seen him at all today.
MISS HACKET. I wonder where he's hiding himself. I must confess he's not the easiest one I've had to handle. He doesn't seem at all keen on the race today. I can't think why.
NICOLETTE. He runs today?
MISS HACKET. Yes. This is his great day!
NICOLETTE. Do you think he will win?
MISS HACKET (*rising*). Think? I *know* it! Though I must confess I have been a little dissatisfied with his training runs. Hardly up to standard, but then I've never been one for statistics. The athlete who is good on training form isn't always first past the tape, you know! You sure you haven't seen him?
NICOLETTE. Quite sure.
MISS HACKET. He's not still in bed?
NICOLETTE. I made his bed half an hour ago. I do not think he was in it.
MISS HACKET. Well, perhaps he's gone for a trot.
    (*Enter* FELIX L.C.)
FELIX. Ah! bonjour! bonjour! bonjour! Welcome to L'Auberge Blanche!
MISS HACKET. Don't be silly. I've been here for days. (*Faces away from him and touches her toes.*)
FELIX. Oh, I am sorry. I did not recognize you behind.
MISS HACKET (*turning to him*). I beg your pardon?
FELIX. But your front—that is more familiar.
MISS HACKET. Don't be disgusting!
NICOLETTE. Have you seen M'sieur Smith, Papa?

FELIX. No.
MISS HACKET. I wanted to give him a work-out. Actually I was a little late, so he may have gone without me.
FELIX. He is in good shape?
MISS HACKET. He will be by the time the race begins.
FELIX. That is not very long.
MISS HACKET (*below* FELIX *to* D.L.). By the way, what is behind that door? (*Indicates the door to the wine cellar.*)
FELIX. That door?
MISS HACKET. Yes.
FELIX. It is a store room.
MISS HACKET. What do you keep in it?
FELIX. Oh, it varies. Sometimes it is one thing, sometimes it is another.
MISS HACKET. It's just that when I was here earlier I heard funny noises coming from in there.
FELIX. You must have been mistaken, madame.
MISS HACKET. Anyhow, I thought I'd better mention it to you. Now I must go and find my baby. If you see him, keep him here till I come back, won't you? (*Exit through the archway.*)
NICOLETTE. Shall we have a look in there, Papa?
FELIX. No, no! No!
NICOLETTE. But some of the wine may have fallen and broken.
FELIX. No, it has not. I looked this morning. Everything is all right.
  (FELIX *goes to* L. *of* NICOLETTE, *puts his arm around her and together they move to* C.)
Nicolette, I have something to tell you. I have turned into a gambler.
NICOLETTE. Papa!
FELIX. It was Mr. Trent who gave me the idea. I have put my money on the race.
NICOLETTE. Oh, no, Papa!
FELIX. I cannot be any worse off than I am now. And I have faith in the English runner. So I put the money on him.
NICOLETTE. To *win?*
FELIX. Of course to win!
NICOLETTE. Oh, no, Papa!
FELIX. Yes! It is good. If he wins, I get four times my money—enough to pay off what I owe and still have some to buy you and Mamma some new clothes!

NICOLETTE. And if he does *not* win?
FELIX. Then I lose my money. But he *will* win! I am certain! And then all will be well!
NICOLETTE. Did you put Mr. Basil's money on as he asked you?
FELIX. Yes. I put on his money. But he made a mistake in what he had written down. I must tell him about it when I see him.
(*Enter* HUMPHREY. *He is wearing dark glasses and a large straw hat which partly obscures his face. He comes to the foot of the stairs.*)
(*Below* NICOLETTE *to* D.R. *of table* C.) Ah! Monsieur Smiss!
HUMPHREY (*to* L. *of table* D.R., *disappointed*). I didn't think you'd recognize me.
FELIX. Miss Hacket has been looking for you.
HUMPHREY. Oh, no!
FELIX. She thinks you should go for a training run.
HUMPHREY. I don't want to see her.
FELIX. But the race this afternoon.
HUMPHREY. Oh, yes—well, I'm ready for that. I just think that any more training would only spoil my performance in the event itself.
FELIX. Yes, that is probably quite true. Nicolette, will you go and see that everything is all right in the kitchen?
NICOLETTE. But why, Papa?
FELIX. Because I want to *know* if everything is all right in the kitchen!
NICOLETTE. All right, Papa. (*She goes off* L.C.)
FELIX. Your wife, m'sieur.
HUMPHREY (*looking quickly* R.). Where? Oh, you gave me a shock!
FELIX. We cannot leave her in the store-room for ever.
HUMPHREY. Why not? I mean why not leave her there a little longer? Just until after I've gone.
FELIX. Gone where?
HUMPHREY (*quickly*). Oh—er—gone to the race. She doesn't like me running, you see. She'd only stop the race somehow.
FELIX. Then we will leave her there! But the other gentleman?
HUMPHREY. Oh, I'd forgotten about him!
FELIX. They are in there together.
HUMPHREY. Yes, I know.
FELIX. But—in there—together—*all* night.
HUMPHREY. Which one of them are you worried about?
FELIX. But this man—who is he?
HUMPHREY. Oh—er—it's her brother.
FELIX. Then we will leave him there, too!

HUMPHREY. Good. Just until after I've—after the race. Then you can let them out.

FELIX. All right. Now, I must go and prepare my radio. I am going to listen to the commentary of your race so I shall know when you have won. (*Exit* L.C.)

(HUMPHREY *goes cautiously and looks off* L. *and* R. *for any sign of* BASIL, *then sits* R. *end of wicker seat.* BRUCHIK *appears from* R. *He passes* HUMPHREY *without recognizing him.* HUMPHREY *whistles to him—and removes his glasses for a moment.*)

BRUCHIK. Ah! I did not recognize you!
HUMPHREY. Is everything prepared?
BRUCHIK (*sitting* L. *of table* C.). Yes.
HUMPHREY. Ready to leave at once?
BRUCHIK. Yes.
HUMPHREY. Then let's go.
BRUCHIK. Have you the stuff with you?
HUMPHREY. Yes. I'm all packed.
BRUCHIK. All right. Nobody is looking. Hand it over.
HUMPHREY. H'm?
BRUCHIK. Quickly! Quickly! Let me have it!
HUMPHREY. Let you have it?
BRUCHIK. Yes—now is the time! Quickly now—before somebody returns. Why are you waiting?
HUMPHREY. I don't know.
BRUCHIK. Then, where is it?
HUMPHREY. H'm?
BRUCHIK. Where is it?
HUMPHREY. Where is what?
BRUCHIK. The stuff.
HUMPHREY. Which stuff do you mean?

(BRUCHIK *whispers to him.* HUMPHREY *is somewhat taken aback by what he hears.*)

Oh, *that* stuff!
BRUCHIK. Where is it?
HUMPHREY. I told you—everything is in my bag.
BRUCHIK. Then go get your bag—quickly!
HUMPHREY (*rising and moving* R.). Yes—yes, of course. Excuse me. I shan't be a minute.

(*He meets* PAULINE *coming on.*)

PAULINE. Oh—hullo!

HUMPHREY. Oh, did you recognize me?
PAULINE. I recognized my hat.
       (*Exit* HUMPHREY *upstairs.* PAULINE *joins* BRUCHIK.)
What's wrong?
BRUCHIK. I am not sure. But I have an unpleasant feeling that we may have blundered.
PAULINE. What do you mean?
BRUCHIK. I would not be surprised if he was not our man at all.
PAULINE. You mean we've made a mistake?
BRUCHIK. We must make certain.
PAULINE. How can we do that?
BRUCHIK. There is one way we can recognize him. You remember the instructions you received? The scar on his right leg?
PAULINE. Yes, of course!
BRUCHIK. If he has got the scar then all is well. But if not, then it will be so much the worse for him.
PAULINE. But the scar is below his knee. How can we manage to see that? We shall have to wait until he changes for the race.
BRUCHIK. That will be too late. We must find a way to see it—now—as soon as he returns. That is up to you.
PAULINE. Me?
BRUCHIK. Of course. I will conceal myself. Quickly, here he comes!
       (BRUCHIK *conceals himself* U.R. *of the stairs.* PAULINE *arranges her hair, as* HUMPHREY *returns.*)
HUMPHREY. Oh. I was looking for Mr. Bruchik.
PAULINE. I'm afraid he isn't here.
HUMPHREY. Oh, I see. Well, I'd better— (*Starts to go.*)
PAULINE. Oh, don't go. Come and sit down here—(*Pause.*)—with me.
HUMPHREY. Well, I really ought to go and—
PAULINE. Just for a moment.
HUMPHREY. Oh, well, just for a moment, then.
       (*He crosses slowly and hesitantly and sits next to her. She closes in at once and he reacts.*)
PAULINE. I can't tell you how brave I think you are.
HUMPHREY. Oh, it was nothing.
PAULINE. You risked your life.
HUMPHREY. Did I?
PAULINE. I always like men who are strong and brave.
HUMPHREY. Do you?

PAULINE. I feel so safe with you. You're so big and protective.
HUMPHREY. Oh, am I?
PAULINE. Why don't you put your arm around me?
HUMPHREY. Somebody might come in.
    (*She now starts to play with his trouser leg in an attempt to get it up above his knee. Each time she does this* BRUCHIK *moves rapidly to* R. *of the wicker seat in a crouched "Groucho Marx" walk. As he arrives there* HUMPHREY *scratches his leg and turns slightly to* R., *and* BRUCHIK *immediately retreats into cover.*)
PAULINE. I do believe you're shy!
HUMPHREY. Oh, no!
PAULINE. Then put your arm around me.
HUMPHREY. Oh, very well. (*He does so. Business.*)
PAULINE. When we both get back to England perhaps we could meet up somewhere?
HUMPHREY. Yes—that would be lovely. But my wife might object. Oh! (*Withdraws his arm.*)
PAULINE. What's the matter?
HUMPHREY. Do you think there's a key-hole in that door?
PAULINE. Why?
HUMPHREY. Oh, I just wondered.
PAULINE. I think you're very sweet. (*Business.*) You don't have to worry. There's nobody in there.
HUMPHREY. Are you sure?
PAULINE. That's where they store food and wine.
HUMPHREY. I wish that was all!
PAULINE. You aren't very friendly! (*Business. She succeeds this time in getting his trouser leg up above his knee.* BRUCHIK *peers closely for a sign of the scar.* BASIL *and* MISS HACKET *enter simultaneously, he from the stairs* R., *she from the archway.*)
BASIL. Ah! a little bit of leg for the photosnap!
    (BRUCHIK *withdraws into cover.*)
MISS HACKET (*to* L. *of* HUMPHREY). I've been looking for you, you naughty boy! Had you forgotten?
HUMPHREY (*rolling his trousers down again*). Forgotten?
MISS HACKET. That very soon now you are running in the five thousand metres. It's time you were getting ready.
HUMPHREY. Well, to tell you the truth, I feel a little giddy.
BASIL (*at foot of stairs*). That'll pass off, old boy, when you get out there on the track.

HUMPHREY. I don't think I ought to run at all.
BASIL. Nonsense! You'll do splendidly. Remember—we're all banking on you.
MISS HACKET. Come along, baby! Time to get changed! (*Pushing* HUMPHREY *towards the stairs.*)
HUMPHREY. Oh, crikey!
BASIL. Now, now! None of that language here! What would your wife think if she could hear you?
 (BASIL *and* MISS HACKET *propel* HUMPHREY *up the stairs.*)
MISS HACKET. Off we go, baby!
HUMPHREY. Oh, to be in England!
BASIL. "Now that April's there"! Never mind all that, come on!
 (*They go off* R. BRUCHIK *comes out of cover to* R. *of wicker seat.*)
BRUCHIK. There was no scar. He is not our man.
PAULINE. Well, no harm has been done.
BRUCHIK. No harm? You call it no harm? He is probably a secret policeman, and if he is he knows too much. We must get him out of the way.
PAULINE. Oh, no!
BRUCHIK. At once! (*Above wicker seat to* U.L. *of it.*) I will have to think of a way. But first, you must get the other one out of the way. I do not want him prying.
PAULINE. I'll do my best.
BRUCHIK. I will leave you now.
PAULINE. Suppose I can't get Trent to leave?
BRUCHIK. You have no alternative. You *must.*
 (*Exit* BRUCHIK *through the archway* U.L. PAULINE *lights a cigarette. After a moment* BASIL *comes on down the stairs. He is wearing a terrible, brightly-coloured sun hat. He sits* L. *of table* D.R.)
PAULINE (*to* L. *of him*). Good afternoon.
 (*He reacts, then assumes a cold air in the way she did to him in Act Two.*)
BASIL. Good afternoon.
 (PAULINE *comes nearer and looks at him admiringly in the same way he did to her.*)
PAULINE (*admiringly*). Lovely!
BASIL. I beg your pardon?
PAULINE. The day! It's lovely.
BASIL. I see.

PAULINE. I say, I'm awfully sorry about the way I behaved yesterday.
BASIL (*grandly*). That's all right. I'd forgotten about it.
PAULINE. You had?
BASIL. Certainly.
PAULINE. May I sit here?
   (*He lifts up his hat and looks at her, then replaces it over his eyes.*)
BASIL. If you like.
PAULINE. You're sure you don't mind?
BASIL. I'm completely indifferent. (*He puts his feet up on to the table.*)
   (*She sits* R. *of table* D.R. *He looks to his* L. *to see if she has gone, then reacts to her on his* R.)
PAULINE. I'm not in the habit of going around talking to strange men like this, you know.
BASIL (*bored*). Really?
PAULINE. Sometimes they don't resist.
BASIL. Really?
PAULINE. No. As a matter of fact, sometimes they find me rather attractive.
   (*She crosses her attractive legs. He peers from beneath his hat and falls off his chair.* NICOLETTE *comes in.* BASIL *collects himself and sits again.* NICOLETTE *is rather upset by the scene.*)
BASIL. I should like some coffee.
NICOLETTE. Oh, very well. (*She goes off* L.C.)
PAULINE (*rising*). I'm going for a bathe.
BASIL. Oh, really?
PAULINE. I bet it's lovely in the water this afternoon.
BASIL. I expect so.
PAULINE. Why don't you join me?
BASIL. I thought you preferred bathing alone?
PAULINE. I can change my mind, can't I?
   (BASIL *clears his throat noisily. She moves up* R. *to the exit, and turns.*)
Shall I expect you?
BASIL (*over-casually*). I'll think it over.
   (PAULINE *goes off* U.R. BASIL *leaps to his feet and dashes off up the stairs.* NICOLETTE *enters from* L.C. *with a tray on which is a coffee pot, milk jug and two cups and saucers. She puts them down on table* C. BASIL *rushes down the stairs again and they meet at* C.)
NICOLETTE (*sarcastically*). Going for a bathe?

BASIL. No, of course not!

(*He runs out* U.R. *after* PAULINE, *and does not succeed in concealing the bathing towel and trunks behind his back.* NICOLETTE *goes* U.S. *and watches him go. Then she moves back to* C., *gets a sudden idea, smiles broadly, takes off her apron, leaves it on table* U.R. *and runs off* U.R. HUMPHREY *appears cautiously from* R. *He is wearing dark glasses and carries a suitcase. He creeps quietly across the stage.* BRUCHIK *comes on from* R.)

BRUCHIK. Aah! Mr. Podmore!

(HUMPHREY *freezes in his tracks.* BRUCHIK *to* R. *of table* C.)

Where are you going?

HUMPHREY. Oh, I—I was looking for you.

BRUCHIK. Here I am.

HUMPHREY. Yes.

BRUCHIK. *Why* were you looking for me?

HUMPHREY. Well, I—

BRUCHIK. You perhaps were going to hand something over to me?

HUMPHREY. Yes, but I—I seem to have mislaid it.

BRUCHIK. That was very careless of you.

HUMPHREY. Well, I must be off now.

BRUCHIK. There is no hurry.

HUMPHREY. Isn't there?

BRUCHIK. No.

HUMPHREY. Oh, well, that's all right then.

BRUCHIK. Come and sit down.

HUMPHREY. I have to get ready for the race.

BRUCHIK. You don't have to pretend with me, Mr. Podmore.

HUMPHREY. But I'm running in the race—I *have* to.

BRUCHIK. There is plenty of time. Come and have a cup of coffee first. It will do you good.

HUMPHREY. Are you sure?

BRUCHIK. Yes. Five thousand metres is a long way. The coffee will keep you awake.

HUMPHREY. Well, actually I—

BRUCHIK (*loudly*). Sit down!

HUMPHREY. I would like some coffee. (*Sits lamely* L. *of table* C.)

(BRUCHIK *sits on the wicker seat and pours two cups of coffee in silence.*)

HUMPHREY. This is awfully good of you.

BRUCHIK. It is nothing. There is some sugar over there. Will you get it for me?
HUMPHREY. Oh, yes, certainly.
  (As HUMPHREY goes L. to get the sugar from side table, BRUCHIK slips some powder into the cup nearest to HUMPHREY. HUMPHREY returns with the sugar. They both solemnly help themselves.)
BRUCHIK (raising his cup). Prosit!
HUMPHREY. Oh yes—thank you. (He raises his cup to his lips and is about to drink, then he speaks instead.) Actually, I really shouldn't drink this, you know.
BRUCHIK. Why not?
HUMPHREY. It's awfully bad for my wind.
BRUCHIK. Nonsense. It will do you good. You will feel much better when you have drunk it.
HUMPHREY. I hope so, because I feel terrible now. (He is about to drink again when he changes his mind.) You know I must thank you for everything you've done for me.
BRUCHIK (patiently). It was nothing. Drink up.
HUMPHREY. Oh yes. (Raises cup again, but again changes his mind.) I shall never leave England again, you know. Not after this.
BRUCHIK. No, I am sure you won't.
HUMPHREY (puts down cup and starts to rise). Well, I'd better be off now!
BRUCHIK (restraining him). I shall be offended if you do not drink your coffee.
HUMPHREY (resuming his seat). Oh, I wouldn't want to offend you.
  (He is about to drink the cup of coffee when MISS HACKET comes on from upstairs. She carries a grip and comes to U.R. of HUMPHREY.)
MISS HACKET. There you are, baby! What's this? Drinking before the big race? Naughty, naughty! (Takes the cup and puts it back on the table.)
BRUCHIK. It is only coffee, Miss Hacket. (He takes up the cup of coffee again, she takes it from him, slaps his hand and puts it on the table.)
MISS HACKET. I don't care. You ought to know better. In any case, why aren't you getting ready for the race?
BRUCHIK. I pulled a leg muscle. I shall not be running in the five thousand metres.
MISS HACKET. Oh, what a pity! I was looking forward to seeing my baby beat you. Come along now, we must be off!
HUMPHREY. But I don't feel very well. I don't think I ought to run today.

MISS HACKET. You mean you'd rather stay here and drink coffee with Mr. Bruchik?
HUMPHREY (*doubtfully*). Well, I don't know.
MISS HACKET. Of course you wouldn't! Come along, baby! Off we go.

(HUMPHREY *rises*.)

BRUCHIK. Just a minute! Perhaps you would allow me to have a flask of coffee sent down to your dressing room for after the race?
HUMPHREY. That would be most considerate, but I can arrange with the hotel to have that done.
BRUCHIK. No, no! I insist! I have a special way with coffee. I will prepare it myself.
HUMPHREY. Well, thank you!
MISS HACKET (*to archway* U.L.). Come along, now!
BRUCHIK. Good luck in your race.
HUMPHREY. Oh. Oh, thank you very much! (*To* MISS HACKET.) Delightful fellow! (*He goes off, returns at once.*) Well, come on, then! (*He pulls* MISS HACKET *off.*)

(*Exeunt* HUMPHREY *and* MISS HACKET. BRUCHIK *quietly empties* HUMPHREY'S *cup of coffee into a plant pot. Then he takes the coffee pot and goes off up the steps* R. FELIX *comes on from* L.C. *to clear the coffee things away.* NICOLETTE *then enters* U.R. *carrying a bundle of clothes.* FELIX *is above* L. *end of table* C.)

FELIX (*to* R. *of wicker seat*). Ah, Nicolette! I have been looking for you.
NICOLETTE. I'm sorry, Papa. I have been down to the lake.
FELIX. What have you been doing?
NICOLETTE. Nothing.
FELIX. You went to the lake to do nothing?
NICOLETTE. Yes, Papa.
FELIX. Couldn't you have done nothing just as well back here? Who was down by the lake?
NICOLETTE. Nobody, Papa.
FELIX. Nicolette, you are not telling me the truth.
NICOLETTE. Yes, Papa!
FELIX. No! I can tell. You have a funny look. What have you got there?
NICOLETTE. Nothing, Papa.
FELIX. That is a very big bundle of nothing.
NICOLETTE. It is—it is Mister Basil's trousers.
FELIX. His trousers! How did you get them?

NICOLETTE. He took them off.
FELIX. What?
NICOLETTE. He was going to bathe. He asked me to press them for him.
FELIX. I do not believe you. (*To* L. *of* NICOLETTE.) Are you sure he knows that you have taken his trousers?
NICOLETTE. Of course!
FELIX. Nicolette—
NICOLETTE (*reasonably*). They needed pressing, Papa.
FELIX (*with a smile*). Why were you cross with him?
NICOLETTE. I was not cross.
FELIX. Did he go bathing with the other lady?
NICOLETTE (*after a pause*). Yes.
FELIX. And that was why you took his trousers, huh?
NICOLETTE. Yes.
FELIX. That was very naughty.
NICOLETTE. Yes.
FELIX. You like Mister Basil, don't you?
NICOLETTE. Yes.
FELIX. Why?
NICOLETTE. I do not know. But he is nice.
FELIX. Do you think he knows that you like him?
NICOLETTE. No.
FELIX. You think that by taking his trousers you will *let* him know?
NICOLETTE. No.
FELIX (*to above* L. *end of table* C). Anyway, what about his wife?
NICOLETTE. He has not got a wife.
FELIX (*picking up the tray*). But he booked a double room.
NICOLETTE. He is not married!
FELIX. Oh, I see. (*With a smile.*) Well, you had better get his trousers pressed, then, hadn't you?
NICOLETTE. Yes, Papa!

(*Exit* FELIX L.C. *with the tray of coffee things. She hugs the trousers for a moment, and is about to go off when there is a noise from behind the cellar door. She moves nearer to listen, then she goes and gets some keys from* L. *and unlocks the door. She opens it and looks in. She screams and runs off* L.C. *with the trousers. Very gently,* AGNES *and the* VISITOR *emerge from the cellar. Both are very drunk in the quiet serious way, and each carries a bottle of wine. The* VISITOR, *a little man, is being held up by* AGNES's *protective arm. He is wearing her hat, she his; and he has a black eye.*)

AGNES. Come along, Hector.
VISITOR. That's not my name.
AGNES. It'll do for now. Let's sit down.
VISITOR. Good idea.
  (*They sit side by side on the wicker seat, he* L., *she* R. *Drinking business: she drinks from her bottle, and as she does so he tries to raise his own bottle to his lips, only to be frustrated in the attempt by* AGNES, *who unconsciously puts a restraining hand on his arm each time she drinks herself. Repeat twice.*)
AGNES. It's lighter out here.
VISITOR. Is it? I don't notice the difference.
AGNES. Why not?
VISITOR. I've got my eyes shut.
  (BRUCHIK *comes down the stairs* R. *with a thermos flask. He goes off* U.L.)
Who was that?
AGNES. I don't know.
  (*Pause. Drinking business again. This time he succeeds in drinking at the final attempt and delightedly has a very long drink, tipping the bottle well up.*)
VISITOR. It was funny my running into you like that, wasn't it?
AGNES. It was not.
VISITOR. Oh?
AGNES. It was far from funny.
VISITOR. Fate, I suppose.
AGNES. Rubbish! I don't mind drinking with you, but don't get sentimental.
VISITOR. I expect it was all planned.
AGNES. I'm sure it was!
VISITOR. It was Destiny.
AGNES. It was not.
VISITOR. I was guided to you by Fate. Fate gave me a push—and there *you* were, waiting to catch me in your arms!
AGNES. It was lucky I was, or you'd have gone flat on your face.
VISITOR. You were meant for me. (*Takes her hand.*)
AGNES. Hector! Don't get sloppy!
VISITOR (*singing*). "You were meant for me—"
AGNES. That's enough of that!
VISITOR (*suddenly and loudly as he sees her wedding ring*). You're married!
AGNES (*alarmed*). What?

VISITOR. Married. (*He points solemnly to the ring.*)
AGNES (*after peering at it closely*). Ooooh, yes!
VISITOR. You're married—and you never told me!
AGNES. Drink up and be quiet! What do *you* care whether I'm married?
VISITOR. Ooooh!
AGNES. What's the matter?
VISITOR. You're a wicked, wicked woman! And I love it!
    (*He snuggles up to her, and they both drink solemnly.* BASIL *comes on from* U.R. *He is without his trousers. Instead he has wrapped a towel around his middle. He comes down* C. *and then sees the two on the seat and tries to cover his legs more adequately.* AGNES *and the* VISITOR *see him.* AGNES *screams.*)
BASIL. S'sh! It's only me!
AGNES. Good heavens! Why are you dressed like that?
BASIL. It's the national costume.
    (FELIX *and* NICOLETTE *enter from* L.C. *They are aghast at what they see.*)
NICOLETTE. You see, Papa? There *was* somebody in there!
FELIX. I do not know how they *got* in there.
BASIL. Where are my trousers?
NICOLETTE. Never mind your trousers!
BASIL. What do you mean, never mind?
NICOLETTE. What are you going to do about them, Papa?
FELIX. Why should I do anything? They seem perfectly content as they are!
NICOLETTE. Aren't you going to ask them how they got in there?
FELIX. Look, the race is about to begin—I am listening to the commentary on the radio.
NICOLETTE. But, Papa—
FELIX. We are going to miss the race.
AGNES. There's an awful lot of noise, isn't there, Hector?
VISITOR. Why don't these people go away and leave us alone?
BASIL (*indicating* AGNES). What's the matter with her?
FELIX. She is not in very good shape.
BASIL. I know she's not a very good shape, but what's the matter with her?
NICOLETTE. Who is that person, Papa?
BASIL. Where are my trousers?
NICOLETTE. I don't know. Who is that person, Papa?

BASIL. Where are my trousers?
FELIX. I don't know.
BASIL. But you *must* know!
FELIX. I was answering Nicolette.
BASIL. Oh, I see.
NICOLETTE. I have not seen him at the hotel before.
FELIX. No. He only arrived last night.
NICOLETTE. What did you say?
BASIL. I said "Where are my trousers".
NICOLETTE. I was not speaking to you.
BASIL. Nobody seems to be speaking to me.
AGNES. Everybody's speaking to everybody far too much! Come along, Hector!
VISITOR. Yes, dear.
(*They rise and move slowly to the cellar door.*)
(*Singing softly.*) "You were meant for me, I was meant for you."
(*They go out and close the door.* AGNES *returns immediately.*)
AGNES. The room service here is dreadful, you know.
(*Exit* AGNES. FELIX *starts to go* L.)
NICOLETTE. Where are you going, Papa?
FELIX. I am going to listen to the race. It will have started by now.
NICOLETTE. You behave as if nothing unusual had happened at all!
FELIX. Well, has it?
NICOLETTE. Of course it has!
BASIL. Yes—I've lost my trousers!
NICOLETTE. Will you shut up about your trousers?
BASIL. Oh, very well. (*He sits* L. *of table* D.R.)
NICOLETTE. Why don't you go and ask them what they are doing in there?
BASIL. Oh, I say! That would be hardly playing the game, you know!
FELIX. The race will be over before I have heard it! I am going. (*He starts to go.*)
BASIL. But where are my trousers?
FELIX. *She* took them! (*Exit* L.C.)
(*A pause.* BASIL *looks at her accusingly.*)
BASIL. Is that quite true?
NICOLETTE. No.
BASIL. *Is* it?
NICOLETTE. Yes.
BASIL. You did take them?

NICOLETTE. Yes.
BASIL. Why?
NICOLETTE. I don't know. I saw you go to bathe with Pauline. I took them.
BASIL. You don't like Pauline, do you?
NICOLETTE. What does that matter?
BASIL. Is that why you took my trousers? Because you didn't like Pauline?
NICOLETTE. Yes.
BASIL. Wouldn't it have been better if you'd taken *her* trousers?
NICOLETTE. She was not wearing trousers.
BASIL. Well, there must have been *something* you could have taken.

(*Enter* PAULINE *from* U.R. *to* U.L. *of* BASIL. *She sees* BASIL's *legs and screams.* BASIL *rises.*)

BASIL. It's not as bad as all that, is it?
PAULINE. I suppose you do know you've lost your trousers?
BASIL. Yes, I did actually. But thanks for telling me. I'm getting used to it now. (*Does a little Highland dance.*)

(*The* VISITOR *appears suddenly from the cellar door but is pulled back again immediately by* AGNES. PAULINE *turns but does not see them.*)

PAULINE. Funny. I thought I heard a door.

(FELIX *rushes on* L.C.)

FELIX. The race is about to begin! (*He rushes off again.*)
PAULINE (*to foot of stairs*). I must go and get ready.
BASIL. Oh, are you leaving?
PAULINE. Yes. I have to go back home—unexpectedly.
NICOLETTE. What a pity!
BASIL. Yes, *what* a pity! I was hoping to see a lot more of you.
PAULINE. I will go and change my clothes and then pack.
BASIL. Can I help you? To pack, I mean.
PAULINE. I think I can manage. Good-bye.
BASIL. We shall see you again before you go?
PAULINE. I doubt it.
BASIL. Of course we will!

(PAULINE *goes off upstairs.* BASIL *moves to* R. *of* NICOLETTE *at* C.)

That wasn't very successful, was it?

NICOLETTE. You do not look very romantic in a bath towel.
BASIL. Don't I? I thought I looked rather dashing. No, I suppose not.
NICOLETTE. But I think you are very sweet.
BASIL. Do you?

>(*They look at each other for a moment, then* FELIX *rushes on again.*)

FELIX. Any minute now they will be off! (*Exit.*)

>(BASIL *glances down at his bare legs.*)

NICOLETTE. Don't you want to hear the race?
BASIL. No fear! I mean no thanks. By the way, your father did put my money on all right, I suppose?
NICOLETTE. Oh, yes. He did. But you had made a mistake in your note inside the envelope.
BASIL. Mistake? What do you mean?
NICOLETTE. It was lucky my father discovered it. Anyhow, it is all right now. My father put it right, and now all is well and your money is on your friend to *win* the race.
BASIL. To *win?*
NICOLETTE. Is that not what you wanted?
BASIL. Of course it isn't! You've lost my money for me!
NICOLETTE. But the race is not over yet. You said yourself that your friend was sure to win.
BASIL. Did I? Nicolette, my friend couldn't win this race if he was riding a bicycle! (*He rushes to the store-room door.*)
NICOLETTE. What are you doing?
BASIL. You'll see! (*He goes into the cellar.*)

>(FELIX *rushes on again.*)

FELIX. They are about to begin! Nicolette, we shall make a lot of money!
NICOLETTE (*subdued*). Yes, Papa.
FELIX (*as he runs off again*). Good luck, Mister Smiss! Good luck! (*Exit.*)

>(*From off* L., *we now hear the vague sounds of a cheering crowd, etc., from the radio. This is maintained until the race is over.* BRUCHIK *comes on from* U.R. *and crosses behind* NICOLETTE *to go off up the stairs. She turns, sees him and screams.* BASIL *reappears pulling the* VISITOR *after him.*)

ACT III] RUNNING RIOT 87

BASIL. Come on, pull yourself together! You've got some running to do. Where are your things?
VISITOR. What things?
BASIL. Your running things, of course!
NICOLETTE. Who is this person?
BASIL. Come on, now. You've got to sober up.
VISITOR. Where's my drink?
BASIL. You've had too much already. Now, try to stand—come on, it's very easy.

(*But the* VISITOR *keeps sagging at the knees.* BASIL *puts him on the chair* L. *of table* C., *and gets to* R. *of him.* NICOLETTE *gets a jug of water from the table* U.R. *and gives it to* BASIL *who flicks some water into the* VISITOR'S *face.* FELIX *runs on.*)

FELIX. They are off! They have started!
BASIL. Too late! (*He empties the jug of water over the* VISITOR'S *head, and sits in despair on the* R. *end of the wicker seat.*)
VISITOR. Oooh! It's raining!
FELIX. Mr. Smiss did not start off too well. At the moment he is hanging back. Oh, he is a clever runner! (*Exit.*)

(*Pause.*)

NICOLETTE. Your friend is not really a runner at all?
BASIL. No. I'm afraid not.
NICOLETTE. Oh—poor Papa.
BASIL. Why poor Papa? I'm the one who's losing money!
NICOLETTE. My father put money on the race as well.
BASIL. Oh, no!
NICOLETTE. If he cannot pay his debts he will lose this hotel. He had not got enough money, so he decided to gamble all his savings.
BASIL. All?
NICOLETTE. Everything. Now he will lose it all.
BASIL (*genuinely*). I'm terribly sorry.
NICOLETTE. Yes. I think you really are. (*With a wan smile.*) You are a very naughty man.

(FELIX *enters.*

FELIX. Mr. Smiss is still there! Why so gloomy? Come and listen to the race! It will be over very soon. (*Exit.*)
BASIL. We'll think of a way out.

(*Enter* AGNES *from cellar, still wearing the* VISITOR'S *hat.*)

AGNES. Ah! there you are, Hector. (*Sees* BASIL.) Young man, you're familiar to me.
BASIL. I wouldn't dream of it.
AGNES. I know that face.
BASIL. Yes. It's mine. It came with the body.
AGNES. And *that's* nothing to write home about!
BASIL. Ah-ha! People in glass houses!
AGNES. You look awful without trousers on.
BASIL. I bet *you'd* look awful *with* them on.

(*Enter* FELIX.)

FELIX. Mr. Smiss is catching up!
BASIL. What?
FELIX. There is time! There is still time! (*Exit.*)
AGNES. Where are your trousers?
BASIL. I don't know.
AGNES. Hadn't you better find out?
BASIL. Mind your own business.
AGNES. Well, really! (*To* L. *of* VISITOR.) Come, Hector. Let's go back to our room.

(*But the* VISITOR *has fallen asleep.*)

Hector! Wake up!
VISITOR (*waking*). Hullo, my flower!
AGNES (*to* BASIL). Hear that? He calls me his flower. (*She is touched by this.*)
BASIL (*to* NICOLETTE). I wonder what kind of flower he means.
AGNES. Come, Hector. You know how to treat a lady. You always say the right thing. (*She is holding his head to her bosom as they go* D.L.)
BASIL. I wouldn't hold his head like that, if I were you.
AGNES. Why not?
BASIL. You might hatch it.

(*They go out into the cellar singing.*)

I shall freeze to death like this.

(*Enter* MISS HACKET *from* U.L. *to below table* C.)

MISS HACKET. Good heavens! Where are your trousers?
BASIL. I mislaid them.

MISS HACKET. Mislaid them, dear boy?
BASIL. Yes.
MISS HACKET. You look like a woman in that thing.
BASIL. Well, you look like a man, so we're quits.
NICOLETTE. Why aren't you at the race?
MISS HACKET. I couldn't face it. I don't think he'll even come in the first three.
BASIL. He'll be lucky if he comes in the *last* three!
MISS HACKET. I hoped he'd pull something out of the bag. They sometimes do, you know. But I'm afraid there's no hope.

(*The* VISITOR *appears from the cellar door and is instantly pulled back again by* AGNES.)

What was that?
BASIL. The cuckoo. It must be three o'clock.

(*Enter* FELIX *excitedly*.)

FELIX. He is going to win!
BASIL. He can't!
FELIX. He has already overtaken most of them!
BASIL. Overtaken them? How can he run so fast?
FELIX. Oh, he is not running fast. But most of the runners are dropping out!
MISS HACKET. Dropping out?
FELIX. Yes. Six already! They suddenly seemed to go faint and dropped out! (*Exit*.)
MISS HACKET. My baby's going to win, after all. And I left him alone down there. He'll never forgive me for this! Never! (*She runs off after* FELIX.)

(*The sounds of the cheering crowd are now much louder from off* L.)

NICOLETTE (*to* R. *of* BASIL). Do you think he might win?
BASIL. I don't think it's possible. *Is* it?

(AGNES *appears from the cellar door suddenly, and is instantly pulled back again by the* VISITOR. BASIL *reacts.*

BRUCHIK *and* PAULINE, *both carrying cases, creep down the stairs* R. BASIL *and* NICOLETTE *watch them go across in front of them and off* U.L.)

(*As they are crossing*.) Hullo! ... Hullo! ... Good-bye! I don't think they recognized us.

(FELIX *rushes on after a loud burst of cheering from off* L.)

FELIX. It is Mister Smiss! He has won! He has won!

BASIL. What?

FELIX. It is true! He has won the race, and all our troubles are over! We have won! (*He embraces* NICOLETTE *excitedly and then moves delightedly to* L.C.)

BASIL. I *can't* believe it! Such things don't happen.

NICOLETTE. But Basil, *you* have won, too!

(MISS HACKET *comes on, weeping,* L.C.)

MISS HACKET. How will he ever forgive me? He won—and I wasn't there to see him. (*She cries.*)

BASIL (*to* C.). There, there! He'll forgive you!

MISS HACKET (*to* L. *of* BASIL). I didn't believe in him, you see. It was very wrong of me. Did *you* believe in him?

BASIL. Yes, of course! I knew he'd win all along! (*Reacts as* NICOLETTE *glares at him.*)

MISS HACKET. He'll never forgive me. I know he won't. (*Cries and is about to be comforted by* BASIL *when she sees his bare legs.*) Why are you still without your trousers?

BASIL. Oh, hell! (*Away to* NICOLETTE.)

(MISS HACKET *to* FELIX *at* L.C., *clear of the archway entrance.* BASIL *stands with* NICOLETTE.)

You called me Basil.

NICOLETTE. Oh, yes. I am sorry.

BASIL. Why sorry?

NICOLETTE. I should call you "Mister Basil".

BASIL. I prefer "Basil"—please.

NICOLETTE. Oh, very well.

BASIL. Look, Nicolette—

NICOLETTE. Yes—Basil?

BASIL. Why don't we get together and have dinner tonight?

NICOLETTE. But I am serving dinner here.

BASIL. Oh, yes. Well, after dinner we could still get together. What do you say?

NICOLETTE. You are a naughty man!

(HUMPHREY *comes on from* U.L. *He is wearing running shorts and shoes, and a flamboyant bath-robe. Around his neck are garlands of flowers. He is breathless and beaming. He comes to* C.)

HUMPHREY. I seem to have won a gold medal.
BASIL. Well done, old boy! I didn't know you had it in you.
HUMPHREY. Neither did I. Oh, I brought back Mr. Bruchik's thermos flask. He gave me some coffee.
BASIL. Did you enjoy it?
HUMPHREY. I never had any. The other runners drank it all.
BASIL. They all drank *your* coffee?
HUMPHREY. Yes. Before the race. There was none left for me.

(AGNES *comes on from the cellar, followed by the* VISITOR *who remains* D.L.)

AGNES (*to* L. *of* HUMPHREY). Humphrey!
HUMPHREY. Good heavens! You're drunk!
AGNES. I'm nothing of the sort, Humphrey Podmore! You haven't heard the last of this, you know. What do you think you're doing all dressed up like—
HUMPHREY. Be quiet, Agnes!
AGNES. What did you say?
HUMPHREY. I said be quiet. You talk far too much. I've always *thought* so, and now I've *said* so.
AGNES. Humphrey!
HUMPHREY. And here you are behaving disgracefully! You'd better go and pack your things. We're going back to England.
BASIL (*up level with* HUMPHREY). To the Little Bruddersford Fruiterers' and Greengrocers' Association?
HUMPHREY. Yes! To the Little Bruddersford Fruiterers' and Greengrocers' Association!
AGNES. So I should think!
HUMPHREY. But not in the *old* way, Agnes.
AGNES. What do you mean?
HUMPHREY. On *my* terms.
AGNES. *Your* terms?
HUMPHREY. Yes.
BASIL. Good for you, Humphrey!
HUMPHREY. You agree with me?
BASIL. Yes, I do!
HUMPHREY. So remember this, Agnes—
BASIL. And *you*, Nicolette.
AGNES. Remember what?
BASIL. That from now on—

AGNES
NICOLETTE } *(together).* Yes?
HUMPHREY
BASIL } *(together).* WE're wearing the trousers!

(*But the others only laugh loudly at the spectacle of* HUMPHREY *and* BASIL *standing together proudly, both wearing* no *trousers.*)

QUICK CURTAIN

PROPERTY PLOT

ACT ONE
Set on table C.
  Cutlery laid for two
  Tray with four large knives, four
    small knives, four forks
  Ashtray
Set on side table L.C.
  Hotel register
  Pen
  Six wine glasses
Table D.L. *and* D.R.
  Ashtrays

ACT TWO
Strike
  All cutlery and crockery
  Briefcase
  PAULINE's suitcase
Set on table U.R.
  Cup and saucer
  Spoon
  Small plate
  Knife
Set on table D.R.
  Cup and saucer
  Spoon
  Small plate
  Knife
Set on table C.
  Two cups and saucers
  Two spoons
  Jug of orange juice
  Two glasses

ACT THREE
Strike
  Everything from tables
Set
  Flowers on all tables
Check
  Suitcase (HUMPHREY) *off* R.
  PAULINE's suitcase (*off* R.)
  PAULINE's coat (*off* R.)
  PAULINE's handbag (*off* R.)
Set on table U.R.
  Jug of water
Set on side table L.C.
  Bowl of sugar

Set off L.
  Six bottles of wine
  Briefcase
  Four suitcases
  Three travelling bags ⎫
  Various parcels   ⎬ HUMPHREY
  Small attaché case   ⎭
  Two glasses of whisky
  Box camera
  PAULINE's suitcase

Set on table D.L.
  One glass
Set on side table L.C.
  One cup and saucer
  One spoon
  One small plate
  One knife
Set off L.
  Four baskets of rolls
  Tray with three dishes marmalade
  Three small jugs coffee
  Three small jugs milk
  Suitcase (AGNES), with under-
    garment inside
  One bottle of brandy
  Suitcase (VISITOR)
Set off R.
  Newspaper

Set off L.
  Tray with coffee pot, milk jug, two
    cups and saucers
  Two bottles of wine
  Garlands of flowers
Set off R.
  Sun hat (BASIL)
  Bathing trunks and towel
  Travelling grip (MISS HACKET)
  Large thermos flask
  Suitcase (BRUCHIK)

PERSONAL PROPERTIES

BASIL
  Cigarette case
  Lighter
  Handkerchief
  Money in envelope
  Wrist watch
FELIX
  Handkerchief
PAULINE
  Handbag

Sun glasses
  Cigarette case
  Lighter
HUMPHREY
  Cigar
  Dark glasses
AGNES
  Handbag
  Visiting card
  Wedding ring

FURNITURE

Wicker seat
Five small round tables
Low oblong coffee table

Seven wicker chairs
Serving table

EFFECTS

Car arriving
Cheering crowd

Commentator's voice

COSTUMES

NICOLETTE
Brightly-coloured full skirt, off-the-shoulder blouse, flat shoes, small white apron (ACT ONE)
Different skirt, blouse, shoes, apron (ACT TWO)
Same skirt as Act One, blouse, shoes, apron (ACT THREE)

FELIX
Tyrolean shirt, trousers, shoes

AGNES
Tweed costume, hat, shoes

BASIL
Sports suit, suède shoes, shirt, tie (ACT ONE)
Sports shirt, slacks, sandals (ACT TWO)
Different shirt, silk scarf, slacks, sandals (ACT THREE)

BRUCHIK
Red roll-collar sweater, fawn trousers, tennis shoes

MISS HACKET
Blue track suit, running shoes

HUMPHREY
   Blue suit, collar, tie, brown shoes, cloth cap. Change into: running shorts, vest, tennis shoes (ACT ONE)
   Grey trousers, jacket of blue suit, shirt, braces, tennis shoes, straw boater (ACT TWO)
   Same as Act Two, then change into: beach robe, tennis shoes (ACT THREE)

PAULINE
   Skirt, blouse, summer coat, shoes (ACT ONE)
   Swimsuit, beach robe, high-heeled sandals, straw hat. Change into: summer dress (ACT TWO)
   Summer dress, or skirt and off-the-shoulder blouse (ACT THREE)

THE VISITOR
   Grey trousers, sports jacket, sweater, cap

LIGHTING

The apparent source of light is daylight from the balcony. The main acting areas are the wicker seat C., tables D.L. and D.R., and the area centre stage.
Suggested colours:
   Cyclorama: Mixture of 16 and 40, with 7 from ground row
   Acting Area spots: 50 or open white
   Sunlight in from balcony: 3
   Other equipment: 50, 51, and 36
   No cues

www.ingramcontent.com/pod-product-compliance
Ingram Content Group UK Ltd.
Pitfield, Milton Keynes, MK11 3LW, UK
UKHW021835210426
5322IPUK00021B/299